SUMMER IN THE CITY

Rock is more than music. It is a way of life. It promises freedom, challenges the establishment, creates a new lifestyle.

'Rock is the story of people's lives, mine included', writes Malcolm Doney. He tells of people and groups, the music, the stars and the fans. But the aim is not just to re-tell the story, but to ask questions. What are these promises of a new life and a new lifestyle? Do they have any basis, any reality? Is this really the way of freedom?

Just when the movement seemed to be played out, the new-wave brought it sharply to life again. So this is not just a matter of history. As an artist and now a journalist with the Christian news magazine *Crusade*, Malcolm Doney believes it is crucial for understanding the world in which we live, for understanding what is happening to *us*, to know what the music, the whole Rock movement, is saying.

An Aslan Lion Book

Rock
Music and Way of Life

SUMMER IN THE CITY

Malcolm Doney

LION PUBLISHING

Copyright © 1978 Malcolm Doney

All rights reserved
LION PUBLISHING
121 High Street, Berkhamsted, Herts

First edition 1978

ISBN 0 85648 085 1

This book is sold subject to the condition that it shall not by way of trade or otherwise be lent, re-sold, hired or otherwise circulated without the publisher's prior consent in any form of binding other than that in which it is published and without a similar condition including this condition being imposed on the subsequent purchaser.

Text set in 11/13 pt Photon Baskerville, printed by photolithography and bound in Great Britain at The Pitman Press, Bath

CONTENTS

Introduction:	The Writing on the Walls	vii
1.	Mutters in the Alley (1945–60)	1
2.	Shouts in the Street (1960–66)	27
3.	Trouble in the Boulevard (1960–66)	52
4.	Summer in the City (1966–69)	69
5.	Summer can't be Beat (1969–72)	98
6.	Fall (1972–)	112

ILLUSTRATIONS

Elvis Presley	5
Chuck Berry	16
The Beatles	33
The Rolling Stones	38
The Who	49
Bob Dylan	58
Frank Zappa	81
Eric Clapton	88
Jimi Hendrix	93
Crosby, Stills, Nash and Young	106
Led Zeppelin	119
David Bowie	124
Johnny Rotten	129

All photographs reproduced by permission of London Features International Ltd.

INTRODUCTION
The Writing on the Wall

One moment Rock music looks as if it's all washed up. Then suddenly something new—like Punk Rock in the seventies—brings the whole scene back to life.

Excitement is once again in the air. The mean, sullen faces of new-wave bands glower from fly-posters on walls and empty shop-fronts. It's like Liverpool during the Mersey Sound boom.

Punk Rock has survived the initial barrage of the media and continues its onward march. In both Britain and America, musical morale is high. Punk, or new-wave (to give it its more acceptable label) is undoubtedly the most creative contemporary development of Rock music.

I was too busy writing the obituary of the Rock culture to notice this at first. Rock had compromised itself, forgotten its quest for real values and settled for an easy life provided, on expense account, by the record industry. But I had badly underestimated the vigour and anger of the growing generation of city-dwellers. They, like me, were scornful of the increasing amount of soft-centre Rock music. Their reply was quick and effective.

SUMMER IN THE CITY

Punk has always been uncompromising, city-bred music. It has been variously described as 'dole-queue Rock', 'anthems of the blank generation' and a 'working-class youth movement'. The music shows the same sharp violence that can be seen in many of the hard kids living in the metropolises of the West. The piston-like rhythm, the harsh vocals are all part of its identification with the seventies landscape.

The lyrics of the songs have little more elegance than the spray-painted slogans on the subway and school walls.

'I is the enemy
I is anarchy'

chanted Johnny Rotten of the infamous Sex Pistols. Synonyms for vacancy and hopelessness form a large part of the Punk/new-wave vocabulary. The names of the groups themselves often reflect a defensive cynicism: The Damned, The Clash and The Boom Town Rats are examples.

Someone once said that Rock was, by nature, a lobbying medium. Certainly in the past it has been used as a means of expressing anger and frustration, even hopes and suggestions. For a while, in the early seventies, Rock music lost sight of that role, but the new-wave has brought it back.

That is not to say we have another protest movement on our hands. The new-wave bands are simply speaking their minds. The victims of their wrath are not just the elderly and the middle-aged, but also younger adults, the product of the sixties youth revolt. The liberal progressivism of that generation is anathema to the new-wave. They see in the tolerance of the sixties a kind of weak-mindedness that has no hope of survival in harder times. Flower power could rest easy in a time of economic stability; Punk Rock grew up in an economic recession; their approach is to meet tough times with equally tough music.

The music and lifestyle associated with the punks has been

INTRODUCTION

violent, obscene and irreligious. It is not my intention to defend Punk Rock or, for that matter, any manifestation of Rock from Bill Haley to The Rolling Stones. I have written this book in order to examine the values (in the widest possible sense) that have been at the root of the popular music of the last twenty or so years; to see how they have affected the music and how the music, in turn, has acted as a catalyst, encouraging changes in attitudes among its young audience.

I do so from a position of commitment. I believe that there is a meaning and order to this world and to man's actions within it, because God created both the universe and its inhabitants. That is not to say that we are perfect or even perfectible beings. Not in the least. The Bible and history speak too loudly for that. All the same, we are capable of good. God's image in us, though tarnished, still shows through. The possibility of music is a result of that. So too is our search for a home in a world made hostile by our alienation from its creator.

The history of Rock 'n' Roll (that is, anything that could be called pop music) is the story of a struggle to come to terms with that hostile world. Rock music is not simply another branch of popular culture. It has shown itself to be perhaps the most significant art form to emerge this century. Not only is it important in itself. It is also a gauge of the shifts in young people's attitudes towards sex, authority, taste, their contemporaries and ethics. It reflects the underlying beliefs which inform their actions and assumptions.

Because Rock is a mouthpiece for youth, the history of the music gives valuable clues as to how and why many children of the post-war era threw out the moral values of their parents. It also shows how that rejection extended to the structures and authority of adult society as a whole.

If old values go and nothing is brought in to replace them, a kind of moral vacuum results. It is not possible for human beings to live either happily or consistently in such a vacuum (a theme dealt with later in the book). Since World War II successive generations of children have realized this and have turned to their contemporaries and to pop music to find both excitement and value.

A rootless and religionless generation sought desperately for some kind of purpose and order in their lives—something their parents couldn't give them. The music was no real substitute for these things but it was, for many, a consuming passion; in some cases an escape; for others a means of identity—'this is *my* music!' That, at least, was how it began. This book traces the development of a collective voice in Rock music and the establishment of alternative values. The vision weakens, fragments and eventually brings us to the anger and confrontation of the new-wave.

I am not a sociologist. Nor am I a professional Rock pundit. But I do love the music. I have, despite my belief that its premises are shaky and its hopes an illusion, identified closely with its challenge to a corrupt and hypocritical establishment, and its espousal of the cause of freedom. Fundamentally, the story of Rock is the story of people's lives, mine included.

This is not a book just for Rock buffs. It is not my intention to expose the intricate workings of the minds of specific performers, nor to assess or vilify their private lives. I simply want to place our recent history in a spiritual and moral context.

It all began long, long ago. I remember it well. I was three at the time . . .

1
Mutters in the Alley
(1945-60)

'Crazy, man crazy!' Just three words marked the start of a social and musical revolution. It was 1953, in the United States of America. 'Crazy, man crazy!' was the first white Rock 'n' Roll record to hit the charts. But the seeds from which the music grew began to germinate in the years immediately following the end of World War II.

The beginnings
Young people were bored and frustrated with the white popular music of the day. In every sense it was the music of a bygone era. The dance-bands and their singers were slick, sophisticated musicians. Their music was dreamy and escapist. Seen now through the permanent soft-focus of nostalgia it seems pleasant and easy. But for the kids of the fifties it was deadly.

Admittedly, one or two of the dance-band vocalists were stepping outside their role as dance-band members and becoming stars in their own right. Singers such as Johnny Ray and young Frank Sinatra were winning a type of adulation formerly the sole property of Hollywood stars.

But dance-band singers had a limited repertoire. Their songs were either romantic tributes of extraordinary sentimentality, dramatic ballads full of Italianate bravado, or witty, foppish novelty songs. They delivered their songs with studied technique, turning out neat, professional performances which had no involvement and no reality.

This was fine for the mums and dads. It was the kind of armchair comfort that had helped them through the war. They were happy to shuffle round the dance-floor to such cosy sounds. But their children were different. They wanted raw excitement—*life*. Though their parents had had to struggle for money and material possessions, times were easier now. The West was just setting out on an enormous consumer boom. Kids took this time of plenty for granted, and wanted their share of it. They had money to spend, time to spare, and they wanted to use them.

One of the first things they did, was to turn the radio tuner-dial in search of something else. They found black music stations playing Blues, Rhythm and Blues, Jazz and Gospel.

This black music, particularly R & B was startlingly different from the music they'd been brought up on. It had a harsh, driving quality. The vocals were rough and uncompromising, the lyrics personal and explicit—whether the subject dealt with was sex, booze or a broken heart. It was everything that white popular music wasn't. Compared with the crooners and their bands, R & B singers looked like wild-eyed broncs alongside trained show-jumpers. Their sound was emphatically black and urban.

It was this contrast that so appealed to American teenage listeners. Their excitement was fuelled by the fact that R & B was often a forbidden fruit. Parents feared the consequences when their children listened to this degenerate, primitive music. Notices like this only heightened their anxieties:

Help Save The Youth of America
DON'T BUY NEGRO RECORDS
. . . the screaming and idiotic words and savage music of these records are undermining the morals of our white youth in America.

Don't Let Your Children Buy, Or Listen To These Negro Records.

'Savage music' describes it well. That was precisely how R & B sounded to ears weaned on more tender music. But the recriminations of parents could do nothing to halt the growing popularity of R & B with the young white audience.

By the beginning of 1953 white groups were starting to include watered-down R & B material in their repertoires. Bill Haley and the Comets were one such group. They had been Country and Western musicians but now they began to play their own versions of R & B songs, such as 'Shake, rattle and roll', changing the words to make them more innocuous, and boosting the rhythm to make it more danceable.

'Crazy, man crazy' was their first hit, and the first white Rock 'n' Roll record to make the charts. From then on Rock 'n' Roll became *the* teenage music. It wasn't Haley's meagre talent that carried the day. His music was crude and lumpy, but it was *new*. For a generation of kids suffocating under the warm blanket of croonings and dance-band music, it was a heady draught of fresh air.

It had the gut-beat and the wildness of R & B that had excited those who turned to the black radio stations for refreshment. Yet, as it developed, it was made increasingly relevant to its white audience. Parents hated it, and that was good news for their children. It meant it was theirs for good.

Apart from the surface ugliness of the music, it was the values Rock 'n' Roll put across that proved distasteful to parents and adults. In place of the sleek good looks of Tony Bennett or Frank Sinatra, came Rock 'n' Roll singers looking like street-corner hoodlums. All the images of Rock 'n' Roll were tough, sinister, brash—even snazzy. There was no sophistication, no polish. It was the poor-quarter with the lid off.

This wasn't all the fault of cuddly Bill Haley. The man of the moment was another, more fearsome, figure; the personification of the mothers' nightmares and the daughters' loves. This was Elvis Presley, Rocker supreme.

Elvis

Elvis was the hero, the god-like personality Rock 'n' Roll needed in order to survive. Had it been left to The Comets, Rock 'n' Roll might have been a mere musical craze of the early fifties, much like skiffle in Britain during the late fifties. But Elvis gave Rock 'n' Roll a new dimension—a sense of style and melodrama.

Elvis was what Haley never could be, a Personality, someone kids could identify with. All his life he remained one of the handful of true superstars in the history of this music. His music was extraordinarily exciting and his charisma immense.

I have to admit he was never really my favourite. I don't much like his voice, though in his raunchier moments, when he was going full steam at something like 'Blue suede shoes', 'Hound-dog' or 'All shook up', even *my* withered, uncharitable heart warmed a little. Elvis was the most effective link between the old, rough quality of R & B and Country and Western and the new, young music. His music appealed to teenagers partly because of the vigour of his performances, but above all because of who he was.

Elvis Presley was young. He was no hardened professional, but a talented Southern boy who'd made good. He came from a similar background to that of his audience, yet he'd rocketed out of it to stardom. His very

Elvis Presley
'The god-like personality Rock n' Roll needed in order to survive'

success, instead of frustrating his fans or making them jealous, confirmed their faith in him. It was, after all, their supreme fantasy to rise out of the daily, penny-pinching, clock-watching drudgery. It was their hard-won money that raised Elvis to his lofty position. What did he give in return?

Elvis gave himself, as the exclusive property of thousands of teenagers in Britain and America. He communicated a personal identity to his girl fans with the combined strength and intimacy of his singing voice on record, fortified by the sensual excitement of his stage-act. He became the dark, handsome stranger many girls dreamed of holding.

He was an object of admiration for the boys, too. Elvis conveyed a tough, masculine image, dominated by a heavy plume of greased-back hair and a semi-delinquent curl of the lip. It was a pose, but the kind that kids looked up to and secretly copied. The gold suits and the gold Cadillac were just what most young men wanted.

Elvis certainly became a myth. He was so surrounded by publicity and legend he seemed far larger than life. This fed his image as the rebel hero. Yet he didn't sing rebellious songs. He wasn't a dissident in the normal sense of the word. Although Rock 'n' Roll has long been considered music of rebellion, Elvis's arrogant pose and stage antics were hardly the stuff revolutions are made of. Nevertheless he was typical of a certain teenage mood in the West. He also became a focus, an image that teenagers could share. It helped to give them a kind of solidarity.

The game—and the rules

Many adolescents believed they'd been born into a set-up. Life seemed to be a gigantic board-game where rigid—though unwritten—rules, a complex of morals, religion, good form, trickery, self-interest and kindness to animals were implicit in the nature of the play. Part of the game was to discover a personal blend of these rules with some help from people such as teachers, parents and clergymen (all of whom had reached their own separate conclusions). It was a game where it was possible to beat other opponents or co-operate with them. But ultimately, no one was the winner.

In previous generations the game had been easier. There had been a God to set the rules. This, according to leading minds of the day, including some theologians, was no longer the case. The suggestion that 'God was dead' wasn't peculiar to this generation; it had a long history. The philosophers of the Age of Reason had thrown God out of the window because they couldn't weigh or measure him.

The notion of agnosticism had over the centuries, filtered down to street-level. By the 1950s and 60s, it was practically a consensus opinion. The Christian God, personal, loving and just, was no longer considered a real option. Certainly Jesus Christ was no longer the central axis of history. Nor was he, for most people, the saviour of the world.

God's seeming absence from human affairs was an extremely important factor in the changing values of young people in the fifties and sixties. In fact it is at the root of the whole swing of western culture this century. Without some such absolute reference point, issues of right and wrong become clouded and relative. Questions of right and wrong were the points of tension in the conflict between parents and children in the post-war years.

The general drift of sentiment at the end of World War II was to make the world free and prosperous, a *better* place. It was a worthy sentiment but one that was rooted firmly in an old order of values. The values were Christian, but by the fifties Christianity was a minority concern.

Despite the fact that they were living in a post-Christian world, many of the attitudes and values of parents and elders bore a visible resemblance to Christian teaching. What puzzled and alienated the younger generation was the fact that these teachers were preaching as truth what they only half-believed. Even those who believed wholeheartedly in what they were saying had only limp, unworked-out reasons for doing so.

Parents told their children: 'No sex before marriage. Respect your elders. Don't steal. Marry for love and for keeps. Never tell lies.' They regarded these norms as beyond all question. They were the foundations upon which life was built. They were *right*.

Their children had a different point of view. They asked the perennial question: 'Who says?' The only reasonable answers to such questions of final authority—God, Jesus or the Bible—were not the instant response. Instead they were told: 'Society says so.' 'I say so.' 'It was the way we were brought up as youngsters.'

Freedom was a prize teenagers desired more than anything. The question of how to cope with it was a minor one. They saw their parents' values as a denial of freedom. And they saw religion in the same light.

The kids were no better, or braver, than their parents in by-passing Christianity as a viable answer to the problems real life posed. Few of them looked at it very closely. Mostly they rejected it as part of the established hypocrisy of their parents' generation. However, having turned aside from the Christian faith, the younger generation was perhaps a shade more honest, and certainly quicker, in seeing the implications of a world without God—it meant 'do what you like'.

This freedom was demanded as a right by young people who felt they were being squeezed into a mould by their parents. In escaping from these pressures by refusing to accept their elders' attitudes and values, they cut themselves off from their parents' culture. They became a rootless, religionless generation. But they felt they were free.

Rock 'n' Roll was a declaration of that freedom. It was

immature, but it said clearly what had to be said—that teenagers were a separate entity.

Wild Southern Rock 'n' Roll
The essential qualities of a Rock 'n' Roll singer were newness and wildness. The singers who appeared in the Southern States of America in the first flush of the music were the wildest and best. Generally they came from working-class backgrounds. Elvis, for instance, came from Tupelo in Mississippi. His prime ambition had been to become a truck driver.

Perhaps the wildest of all the Rock 'n' Rollers was a black man, Little Richard. If Elvis was sensual, Little Richard was hysterical. He was a black peacock. With hair pushed high off his head he would pound his piano in a fury, screeching his way through songs like 'Tutti frutti', 'Long tall Sally', 'Lucille' and 'Girl can't help it'. Ounce for ounce of pure adrenalin, he remains the most hair-raising and exciting of the Southern Rockers. There was no explicit rebellion in his songs. They were all about the reckless good-times, the kind that teenagers dreamed about but which their parents forbade.

Jerry Lee Lewis was another wild man. Like many other white Rock 'n' Roll singers, he began by singing Country. But he'd soaked up a good deal of black musical influence and although he later returned to his origins, his Rock 'n' Roll songs were classics. He too was a piano player who beat, rather than played, his instrument. He had a persistent, if unaesthetic, gravel voice which would rip through the mashed piano chords. He sounded nasty—and the kids loved it. His most memorable hits were 'Whole lotta shakin' goin' on' and 'Great balls of fire'.

These, along with Elvis, were the tough, macho Rockers. They were rumbustious, sensual and mean.

Sex

One element of Rock 'n' Roll which passed me by at the time (I was only seven or eight) was sex. It was the ingredient which, apart from noise, caused the most controversy. Pundits, parents and preachers howled furious damnations on what they thought were overtly sexual actions—Elvis's gyrating hips, for example. Both Rock 'n' Roll's enemies and its champions have said the music was principally about sex. The music said 'fornication', even if the words were about holding hands and kissing.

Rock 'n' Roll's detractors claimed that the music was evil. They said that its primitive beat and the posturings of its performers encouraged an irresponsible attitude towards sex. Rock's supporters argued that of course the music was about sex. It had stripped away the hypocritical veneer of romance and replaced it with the real thing. Others talked of Rock 'n' Roll as an unashamed celebration of uninhibited orgy. Jeff Nuttall, for example, in *Bomb Culture* talked about Elvis as a god: 'He was the idol in a literal sense, a deity incarnate in the old primitive pattern, the catalyst of a rediscovered appetite for community in its fundamental form, orgiastic ritual.'

Poor Elvis! He was cast in so many roles, this time as a sort of fertility god. He was hailed as anything from an unconscious leader of a movement of sexual and social liberation to a manufactured turn-on for adolescent girls.

Sexual freedom and sexual explicitness have been an obsession in the West for much of this century. I'm certain that the sexuality of Rock 'n' Roll was less of an issue than some claim. I don't want to soft-sell Elvis or any other of the Rockers. Obviously his voice was more intimate and sensual than either dance-band crooners or singers of high opera. It would be foolish to suggest that the notorious pelvis which Presley shifted with such style had no erotic connotations. But it is too simple to say that Rock 'n' Roll was only sexual.

The adolescent screams, the other manifestation produced by Rock 'n' Roll—have been described as a kind of sexual hysteria. Some said it was the direct result of cynical manipulation by performers. Others saw it as a redirection of the sexual feeling of teenage girls. There's an element of both. But mostly it was a conscious response to individual performers and their music.

In an interview, Brian Epstein, The Beatles' manager, quoted the example of a girl at a Beatles' concert. She was in mid-scream when her handbag fell off her lap. Epstein said: 'She stopped screaming, bent down, picked it up, had a quick inspection to make sure nothing had fallen out or got broken, put it back safely between her thigh and the edge of the seat so it wouldn't fall again, put her hands to her head, and started up again.' As Brian Epstein said, 'That's not hysteria, that's self expression.'

George Melly, the Jazz singer, tells a similar story of two girls he heard discussing whether to scream for the support act or save their lungs for The Beatles. The same, I'm sure, was true of the Rock 'n' Rollers.

Black music was always much earthier than Rock 'n' Roll. Many R & B singers were fairly explicit in their sexual references in songs. In Blues terminology, Rock 'n' Roll had always been synonymous with love-making, hence this famous line: 'Rock me baby, till my back aint got no bone.' But the term changed and when Rock 'n' Roll emerged as a musical form it had lost its sexual overtones. In fact Rock 'n' Roll singers would sometimes water down the lyrics of black songs in order to make them more acceptable to a white audience.

For instance, the original version of 'Shake rattle and roll' recorded by Joe Turner, a black artist went:

'Well you wear low dresses
The sun comes shinin' through

I can't believe my eyes
That all of this belongs to you.'

That was too risqué for the white market of the fifties so Bill Haley's hit version ran:

'You wear those dresses
Your hair done up so nice
You look so warm
But you heart is cold as ice.'

It could be argued that cosmetic changes of that kind do nothing to change the basic meaning of the song. But for a new audience, unaware of the original versions, the cleaned-up songs were taken at face value. Songs like these were good-time, exciting romps. The hard facts of co-habitation, very relevant to the adult black audience, simply didn't relate to a white teenage one. Necking and the occasional late-night fumble were the limits of general experience for the fifties market and Rock 'n' Roll had much more to do with that.

The arrogant stagey sexiness of singers such as Elvis were much glorified by advocates of sexual freedom and condemned by the conservatives. Some teenage girls were undoubtedly turned on by it, and screamed. Others were affected more by the infectious bravado that came from a new-found identity with other kids.

Many young people, while rejecting in principle their parents' idea that sex before marriage was wrong, didn't do anything about it. They seldom went 'too far'. They feared pregnancy, had limited knowledge of the facts of life and held a sneaking respect for their parents' moral directives. Their support for freedom was often only a matter of theory. Many young men itched for the freedom to be able to sleep with whoever they wanted—but the weight of conventional propriety was too heavy for any but the boldest to shrug off.

Agressive sexuality, undeniably a *part* of Rock 'n' Roll, had a serious part to play in reflecting the sexual aspirations of the fans. One facet of Elvis's image was that of the arrogant stud. It appealed to boys and girls alike. To the girls he was the dominant male. To the boys he was the man they wanted to be.

Violence and delinquency

Rock 'n' Roll was city music. The vast majority of the record-buying public lived in the cities and Rock 'n' Roll was theirs. Like R & B, which had played such a large part in its musical heritage, it was a hard, electric city-bred noise.

One top city Rocker was Eddie Cochran. His records have an echoey urban sound about them and his songs were filled with references to the perennial problems of a young city-dweller. 'Summertime blues' is the archetype.

> 'My grandfather told me, "son you've got to earn some money
> If you want to use the car to go around next Sunday"...
> ... He said, "you can't use the car 'cos you didn't work late."'

Rock 'n' Roll, of course, has never been just about words. Its qualities have been wrapped up in both the music and the style. Eddie Cochran managed to combine those things and produce a few dynamic moments in his short life (he died in 1960).

Because he fits in so neatly with all my theories about Rock 'n' Roll as a vibrant, urban electric Folk music, I ought to like him a lot. As it is, I don't. Eddie Cochran's music always seemed all grit and muscle and not a lot else.

Rock 'n' Roll's harsh city sound blended well with the city teenager's attitude to living. It was fast, bustling and hard:

like street-life in the big cities of Britain and America.

Teenage resentment grew into violence and crime. In the States there were mutually hostile regional gangs with over-elaborate names: the Dragons, the Rebels, and Grand Gangsters Incorporated. In Britain there were the Teds, gangs of elegant but nasty street punks. As Rock 'n' Roll developed it became their music. Gangs were a symptom of the times and have wrongly been linked with Rock 'n' Roll in a cause-and-effect equation: that is, Rock 'n' Roll was the cause of delinquency.

The fact that there was a wave of delinquency in the post-war years is undeniable. The reasons for it were manifold. Teenagers were bored because there was nothing interesting for them to do. The city environment was restrictive and brutal. They had no cultural focus or identity because they had cut themselves off from their elders' attitudes and pursuits and had therefore caused a break in the normal cultural continuity. Generally the work they did was automatic, repetitive, uncreative and without prospects. These jobs paid relatively well, but there was little worth spending the money on. Spiritually these teenagers were arid. They had no God, or if they did, gave him little regard.

Delinquency—like sex—was added to the black list of Rock 'n' Roll's implicit characteristics. This has always seemed to me a shallow view—short on understanding and long on hysteria. There was a history of anti-authoritarianism, physical assaults, theft and vandalism by young people long before Rock 'n' Roll arrived on the scene.

When Rock 'n' Roll came, delinquency—naturally enough—didn't vanish. Dance-halls and clubs where Rock 'n' Roll was playing became the arenas for vigorous brawls and vandalism. These kids were rough, and if they were out for kicks, rough it was going to be.

Colin Fletcher, in the British journal *New Society*, gives a first-hand account of one of the riots that took place all over Britain following the showing of Bill Haley's film *Rock Around the Clock*. This violence strengthened the idea that Rock 'n' Roll and delinquency were inextricably linked: 'Soon couples were in the aisles, copying the jiving on the screen. The "bouncers" ran down to stop them. The audience went mad, chairs were pulled backwards and forwards, arm rests uprooted in an unprecedented orgy of violence.'

Trouble certainly followed the music around—but this was not due simply to the nature of the music. Rock 'n' Roll encouraged people to get to their feet, dance, and become involved in the music. You could call that disorderly—or you could call it fun. It was exciting music, and those with aggressive tendencies used it to focus their violence, but it was never inherently violent.

Chuck Berry

It's easy to tie the bull-like agression of the wilder Rockers to the discontent of teenagers. The explosiveness of the music was for its audience an exchange in kind for their own inarticulate feelings. But that wasn't the only way it was expressed.

Chuck Berry did it differently. Unlike many of the other Rockers, he wrote his own songs. In my opinion he was the first *writer* to come out of Rock 'n' Roll. He's certainly my all-time favourite Rock 'n' Roll singer. He was unique. He wrote outstanding 'miniatures' of contemporary American life. He maintained an affectionate regard for the detail of day-to-day experience that really made his songs come alive. He was black, lean and canny, with a very individual R & B style of guitar-playing.

It may well be my literary interest that prejudices me in his favour. He wrote such strong lyrics. For instance, his

Chuck Berry
'More than anybody, he pinpointed the feelings and frustrations of adolescent life'

song about a teenage marriage, 'You never can tell', was packed with phrases and jargon that summed up a segment of the American life-style: an apartment where 'The coolerator was crammed with TV dinner and ginger ale'; and a specific taste in cars—'They bought a souped-up Jidney, was a cherry-red '53.' It was Pop-culture poetry, and it wasn't given the respect it was due until the rise of Pop art and Pop poetry in the sixties. The Liverpool poets of that time came near it but even their work was a pale pastiche of Chuck Berry—and he had music, too.

Chuck Berry wrote teenage anthems. 'Roll over Beethoven' was a proud declaration of the power of Rock 'n' Roll. Teenagers who'd had 'good music' shoved dogmatically down their throats from birth immediately identified with this one. 'Jonnie B. Goode' was a guitar-picking Folk-hero who 'played guitar like he was ringing a bell'.

Berry, more than anybody, pinpointed the feelings and frustrations of adolescent life. His audience knew and experienced what he was singing about. Take 'Sweet little sixteen' for instance:

> 'She's got the grown up blues
> Tight dresses and lipstick
> She's sporting high heel shoes
> Oh, but tomorrow morning
> She'll have to change her trend
> And be sweet sixteen
> And back in class again.'

That was a fair evaluation of a teenager's life. Many school kids, as they grew older, found themselves living a dual life. In school, then out on the street. It was on the street and around the juke box that they really came alive, as Chuck Berry says in 'School days'.

Northern Rock

Buddy Holly didn't come from the Northern States, neither did the Everly Brothers. Geographically they came from the South. Musically they were somewhere in the middle. The South was the home of a harder, wilder Rock 'n' Roll; the North gave birth to a smoother, less obviously rebellious, kind of music.

Buddy Holly's songs were softer and more appealing than those of, say, Little Richard, but they had more oomph than Paul Anka's. 'That'll be the day' was perhaps his toughest song. Most of them were pleasant but innocuous. They were insubstantial, like those cheap plastic footballs which bobble about in the wind.

The Everly Brothers were much better. They are usually thought of as a fifties group, yet they didn't achieve real success until later. They had strong Country roots, but they managed to be more than just Country-and-Western-with-a-beat. Their harmonies had such a keen edge, they bit right into your heart.

The emphasis in Northern Rock was on the silky, multi-part harmonies of vocal groups, or the smooth tones of solo 'Rock' ballad singers. The Platters, The Chantels, Danny and the Juniors, Paul Anka and Pat Boone are all part of this branch of Rock 'n' Roll. This music was closer to the white musical tradition than to Blues or Country. The black influence came in the form of Gospel, with a soft call-and-response style of singing in the vocal groups. Although the music was very 'white', there were a number of black groups.

I hate it and love it in turn and simultaneously. It was at the same time so crass and so precisely American. It neither rocked nor rolled you, you floated on it, dreaming of the teenage myths it sang about. It was preoccupied with a caricature of elements of the American teenage lifestyle—what Rock pundit Nik Cohn calls 'high school'.

On the surface the music and the artists seemed to fall into a more-or-less conventional showbiz mould. The songs seemed to be a glorification of materialism and the American way of life. This was cleaned up Rock 'n' Roll. These shoobey-doo-wah, tight-harmony extravaganzas were safe excitement for the timorous and they settled snugly alongside the great American 'isms'—materialism, racism, sexism, and imperalism.

That was what it *seemed* like, and it was true to some extent. Kids in the fifties rarely had any quarrel with either politics or materialism. Teenagers were intent on being free and being able to enjoy their pleasures free of restriction. They didn't challenge their parents' materialism for what it was, they simply wanted their share. It was the rebellious 'prodigal son'—if you remember the story—all over again.

In some respects the teenage attitude to materialism went further than that of their parents. It was a matter of creating a greater potential freedom. With a car, *and* money, *and* hi-fi equipment, *and* good clothes, there was nothing that couldn't be done.

'High school' was essentially youthful. It was a celebration of youth. All the sentiments of the songs supported the notion that being young was a serious business. Such songs lent an identity, a permanence to adolescence. The music promoted the feeling that to be sitting in a classroom was to be *somewhere*, not just passing through a phase, as parents and leaders insisted. Somehow it made being a teenager seem *heroic*.

Teenagers convinced themselves that 'reality' was a world beyond parental restraint and limited to the amount of what could be possessed and experienced. Rock 'n' Roll sustained this illusion. Despite its communication with real people, and some real understanding of human actions, Rock 'n' Roll was a pedlar of dreams. Its 'reality' was less than the real thing. It used the word 'love' but destroyed its meaning. 'I love you' came to mean, 'I want you'—and appetite isn't enough.

It wasn't until later that young people began seriously to consider the real meaning of human relationships and the mindless rat-race that materialism fostered. However, a number of people on both sides of the Atlantic anticipated some of the changes that were to overcome this generation and its successors.

The Angry Young Men

The Beats, in America, appeared in the late forties. They were an informal collection of poets and writers scattered throughout the States. They were a generation older than the Rock 'n' Rollers. A number of them had seen war service of one kind or another; they were in their twenties at the beginning of peace-time. They were angry and incredulous at the human capacity for hatred and slaughter that the war had shown. They were sick at the worship of money and technology that the post-war years produced.

In disgust, they turned away from the conventional way of life, cast aside the restrictions of bourgeois morality and cultivated a free lifestyle. Poets like Allen Ginsberg and writers like Jack Kerouac left the cities and rambled into the heart of America in an attempt to discover themselves, and to find values that related to their own experience.

They were, in Jack Kerouac's words, 'an informal spiritual answer to the problem of an honourable survival in a violent age'. Their writings poured obscenities and anger on the heads of their fellow countrymen. They experimented with drugs, they dabbled in Zen, and immersed themselves in Jazz—but they found no solutions. They were too committed to the search to look for the answers.

In Britain, in the mid-to-late fifties, another informal collection of writers developed. In their novels and plays, they insulted and poked fun at the systems and circumstances of British society. The revolt of these Angry Young Men was more a matter of literature, than of lifestyle. They were preoccupied with the class structure and its evils.

It was fashionably described as the liberation of the working class, but again it was a middle-class movement which never really reached the roots of working-class discontent. If anything, it was the intellectual liberation of the grammar school pupils—not a bad thing in itself. The novels of John Braine, John Wain and the plays of John Osborne exposed the dilemmas of a section of society no one had paid much attention to before.

In the fifties there were anti-bomb movements, too. In Britain the Aldermaston marches began. Middle-class idealism found a means of organized expression. It was a political protest focussed on the nuclear problem, and not a revolt of lifestyle. There were vague rumblings, though. The romantic image of the Beats had filtered through and the visual trappings of Beat-dom were in evidence amongst the marchers—beards, sloppy jumpers and sandals. Like the Beats, the marchers felt that technology had turned monster at the hands of power-crazy politicians. But they differed from them in clinging to the thread of a belief that governments could be reasoned with.

All of these 'romantic' movements, faded and died by the sixties. Nevertheless, they were the political and social foundations on which the Civil Rights protesters, the Vietnam demonstrators, the Folkies and the Hippies were to build a new tottering edifice of romance in the next decade.

British Rock 'n' Roll

The Angry Young Men and the Aldermaston marchers were not part of the upsurge of Rock 'n' Roll. But that didn't mean that Rock 'n' Roll music failed to reach Britain. On the contrary, British audiences were invaded by Rock 'n'

Roll—much as their forebears, the Thanet villagers, had been by a series of armies. But it wasn't fire and the sword this time, it was Bill Haley. Who needed fire and the sword with Bill Haley's film *Rock Around the Clock* causing riots up and down the country?

The cultural situation in Britain was similar to that of America at the end of the war. Affluence was slower to come, and technology didn't seem so magical—it always looked somehow shabby and industrial. There was the same discontent among teenagers and the same desire for real music and for freedom. There wasn't at this stage an indigenous black population and so there were no musical roots for British youngsters to borrow. They relied on American imports.

But British teenagers weren't going to content themselves with listening to American music. They wanted a piece of the action. The only popular musical roots they had were Folk music and music hall, and they weren't tough enough, so they copied the Americans.

Elvis was the model. British singers doggedly imitated both his image and singing style. Their music was full of vapid, second-hand menace. There was Tommy Steele, a regular cockney sparrow who tried to be moody but could not stop grinning. He started what was to become a well-worn path from Rock 'n' Roll into family entertainment. Cliff Richard, like Tommy Steele, began as an Elvis carbon. But he looked better, sang better and had more of the style and the image. He really was the biggest of the British Rockers. But he never quite met with the raw edge of Rock 'n' Roll and soon found a place as a quality family entertainer.

Almost as big as Cliff were The Shadows, his backing group. They churned out a series of instrumental hits which had a profound influence on the growing hordes of adolescent guitar-pickers all over the country. There was also Adam Faith, whose singing style was close to Buddy Holly's and who used to jerk his strangulated way through such hit songs as 'What do you want?'. For sheer image, perhaps Billy Fury came out best.

Naturally the British inclination for eccentricity was freely indulged in Rock 'n' Roll. There were fiendish stunt-artists like Screaming Lord Sutch and Wee Willie Harris, and manager Larry Parnes's stable of wonderful names: Marty Wilde, Vince Eager, Duffy Power, Johnny Gentle, and others. But British Rock was always sub-American.

There were no British song-writers of the stature of Chuck Berry or Eddie Cochran, no one with the right feel for a telling image or a barbed hook-line. What was needed were short, hard-driving simple songs that could appeal to teenagers without being banal. It wasn't until The Beatles arrived, with their long-felt enthusiasm for and knowledge of American music, black and white, that any British song writers managed to succeed.

Skiffle, a derivation of American folk music, swept Britain with its home-made instruments, tea-chest bass and washboard. Then came Trad Jazz, an emasculated version of New Orleans Jazz, played to the accompaniment of much beer swilling and loosely linked to the middle-class anti-bomb mob. Both were played into the ground in a short period.

But I haven't really mentioned the Teds. History has identified the Teds with Rock, especially since the many Rock 'n' Roll revival clubs in Britain make a point of dressing in true Ted style. They were called Teddy Boys because of the mock Edwardian cut of their long drape jackets which they wore with narrow drainpipe trousers, bright socks, thick crepe-soled shoes and string ties.

They originated in the rougher areas of London before the advent of Rock 'n' Roll. But when Rock 'n' Roll arrived they took it on as their personal property. They were the storm troops in the generation war. They hated with a big

H. They hated older people, their jobs, authority and do-gooders. The Teds had a real chip-on-the-shoulder mentality. They did what they liked and their violence scared people badly.

They were bored a lot of the time, so if they weren't clustered round the juke box, they went looking for trouble. There was no excitement in their lives, so they had to fabricate it. They weren't products of the music, they adopted it as part of their life-style because it fitted in with their own curious values. The music, like their clothes, was a badge that meant acceptance in a closed fraternity.

Inevitably, although the Teds claimed Rock 'n' Roll as their own and remained loyal to it long after everyone else had moved on, the Rock 'n' Roll audience in Britain was bigger than they were. Some of the Teds' style—the greased hair and the drainpipes—rubbed off on young Rock 'n' Roll fans, but less of the violence.

Demise

There were many different styles and different emphases within Rock 'n' Roll. It was a mixture of musical influences, and its audience was mixed too. The teenagers who loved it had no clear direction. By overturning their parents value systems, they'd left themselves in a moral vacuum. Their own values were confused. They had little to hold on to. The only thing they could clutch at was the reality of their own experiences and their dreams of freedom. Rock 'n' Roll had brought teenagers closer to their dream. The music proved to be a powerful medium. It was responsible for reviving a flagging record industry. It united the discontented young and made them aware they were no longer individuals but part of a whole generation—youth.

The success of Rock 'n' Roll made manufacturers aware of the existence of a youth market. They started to manufacture products specially for them. So the fifties saw clothes, hairstyles, magazines, soft drinks and TV programmes tailored specifically for teenagers. That in itself was one of the great changes of the decade.

In a way these were merely logical extensions of Rock 'n' Roll, but they had their own significance. The fact that teenagers were being treated differently from adults, that they were recognized as a separate entity, gave them an enormous boost of confidence. They had won a skirmish. Also the production of teenage goods accentuated the visual and stylistic differences between young and old. The generation gap widened.

As teenagers grew in self-confidence, their tastes became more refined. Although they still saw Rock as entertainment and not art, they began to realize its potential as a weapon. It was their one chance of making an impact on adult society. They had already driven a wedge into the adult-dominated media. They had a voice.

So far this voice had only been a mutter, but it was growing louder. Out of a sulky resentment and dissatisfaction came something more positive: the search for an authentic experience, something they felt was absent from the lives of their elders.

But Rock 'n' Roll itself was dying. It had started off wild and a bit crazy, but it ended placid and docile. In the States, radio stations quietened Rock down by neglecting the wilder records and playing the soft melodies of the North.

The army of Elvis deputies, Tab Hunter, Pat Boone, Fabian, Bobby Rydell and the rest, took over the radio waves and sang their cheap imitations. After an all-too-brief interlude, when it looked as though Rock 'n' Roll could keep itself out of the clutches of showbiz, Tin Pan Alley's tentacles grabbed hold. The music business churned out gallons of easy-listening suburban Rock 'n' Roll. It was mannered and spiritless, all idiot sentiment and puffed-up drama.

In Britain, dependent on American hits to supply its own singers, things went the same way. Rock 'n' Roll slipped away and died. But although the music was finished, teenagers weren't. The kids in the street weren't satisfied with the nonsense that came seeping through the radio. They had been given a glorious glimpse of excitement and freedom. They weren't going to leave it there. They were still buying records, but as the explosive welcome they gave The Beatles indicated, they were just biding their time, waiting for a new set of heroes.

2
Shouts in the Street
(1960-66)

The period of the early to middle sixties saw teenagers continuing the fight for freedom. As yet they lacked an ideology, but by this time there were new heroes—The Beatles, The Rolling Stones and others—to take up cudgels on their behalf.

The teenagers of the fifties were, obviously, twenty-year-olds in the sixties. Many of them still listened to Rock. At the same time a new 'generation' of kids was becoming teenagers, to the accompaniment of new sounds. I was one of them. We'd grown with the sound of Rock 'n' Roll in our ears, but as adolescents we wanted music that would tell of *our* experiences. That music was called Pop.

Rock 'n' Roll had been a powerful force in the media, but groups like The Beatles now took over. A growing demand for freedom was working its way into the media and the arts, breaking the old barriers of what was acceptable. Figures of authority were hauled off their pedestals and subjected to laughter and scorn. The Beatles and The Stones looked well against that background.

Youth became defiant. New styles of hair and clothes were

the visible symbols of rebellion.

Musically, the sixties began as the fifties ended—limply.

Elvis lost some of his grip. He released a series of flabby ballads which bore no comparison with the muscular records of his early career. The other big-league singers of the fifties were silent. Jerry Lee Lewis faded, Chuck Berry was in jail, Buddy Holly was dead, and before 1960 ended so was Eddie Cochran.

The scene was dismal. Unfortunately the Rock 'n' Rollers, good as they were, lacked the flexibility, and in some cases the desire, to develop their music. Rock 'n' Roll itself was limited in its emotional range and its musical possibilities. Something extra was needed. Yet no one seemed capable of providing it.

One or two artists provided a little life in the musical doldrums between 1959 and 1963. Neil Sedaka was easily the liveliest. He wrote good, commercial Pop songs like 'Oh! Carol' and 'Breaking up is hard to do'. His melodies were well judged, light and bouncy and they focussed on perfectly weighted hook lines. Sedaka was perhaps the first Pop figure.

Roy Orbison and Del Shannon also made good during this time. Roy Orbison would let rip his fine howling voice on a series of breast-beating songs of agonized passion. I found it a bit gruesome, but he was the best of a poor offering. Del Shannon was a minor leaguer but there was an appealing teenage element in his songs—small-town stories of jiltings and crushes. 'Little town flirt' is one that immediately springs to mind.

This trickle of good music wasn't enough to constitute a new direction in Pop. Sedaka, Orbison and Shannon could all sing, and they all made impressive records. But none of them was rebellious or exciting enough to catch the imagination of the young. None of them was going to lead the battle against the older generation.

R & B rediscovered

But change was on the way. In Britain, in peoples' homes and in seedy clubs R & B was being rediscovered.

Generally, Britons had no access to R & B records prior to and during the Rock 'n' Roll era. They took and accepted American Rock 'n' Roll but they hadn't discovered its roots. This was one reason why British Rock was so weak; it didn't have enough to work from. All it had was hybrid Rock 'n' Roll.

However, by the end of the fifties and beginning of the sixties, R & B records were arriving in increasing numbers. They were still collectors' items, but those who were keen could get them. Those youngsters who did discover R & B at this time were overjoyed. This was real, exciting, personal music in contrast to the artificial, frothy Pop-jingles of the charts.

The number of R & B fans grew. Newcastle, Liverpool and London were the kind of cities that fostered this new interest. They were international ports and access to imported records was easier there than elsewhere. It is no coincidence that the groups who had so much to do with the new wave of music—The Beatles, The Rolling Stones and The Animals—came, respectively, from Liverpool, London and Newcastle.

R & B found a new type of fan. He was reasonably educated, often from a middle-class background. He took the music seriously, but not too seriously.

The musicians amongst them seized on R & B songs, chewed them up and spat out their own versions. As LeRoi Jones, a black writer, said of British R & B groups: 'They take the style of black Blues, Country or city, and combine it with the visual image of White American non-conformity ... and score heavily. These English boys ... have actually made a contemporary form.'

In their early days as a group The Beatles devoured every

morsel of music to come their way. Mostly it had an R & B flavour. Blues, Gospel, Soul or Rock 'n' Roll, were all eaten up. The album recorded in those early days in Hamburg gives a clear picture of the raw diet they were feeding on. At that stage, afficianados of black music were a close fraternity, as John Lennon said: 'We felt very exclusive and underground in Liverpool listening to all those old-time records. And nobody was listening to any of them except Eric Burdon in Newcastle and Mick Jagger in London.'

Despite all these influences, Lennon and McCartney's own songs were much more than mere hotch-potches of everyone else's material. Their work bore their own individual stamp. It was fresh, new and inventive. The music was tough but compelling and melodic. It was so obviously 'quality' that it would have been successful anyway. But the excellence of the music doesn't account for the fact that The Beatles became more than hugely famous, they became *cosmic*.

Just as at the beginning of Rock 'n' Roll, the timing was perfect.

A new mood

There was a new spirit abroad. It was best seen in Britain which, after all, The Beatles hit first. It argued with, and questioned all the old established attitudes. And this time it wasn't just the kids who were responsible.

Government in Britain was stable but hidebound. Harold MacMillan's Conservative government had been in office for nine years in 1960 and was to see four more before it was ousted. There was a consumer boom and a background of economic stability. On the surface things were settled and stable. 'You've never had it so good' was the government's slogan of the day.

But underneath there was an undercurrent of unrest, a desire for change and action. If that did not prepare the way for The Beatles, it certainly gave them a timely relevance that helped their success.

The spirit of the Angry Young Men was still alive in the sixties. There was a strongly critical attitude among young intellectuals. Many of them found work in the media—in TV, film, journalism and photography. They were free thinkers, unwilling to kowtow to the establishment. Television was still relatively young, and the sixties was a boom time.

These bright young TV producers, critics and journalists didn't keep a respectful silence in the presence of authority. On the contrary, they poked them and asked tough questions. They showed the public that these people weren't above reproach and that their mystique was often ill-founded.

Satire grew out of this de-bunking, and during the early sixties it, too, experienced a boom. Established ideas and public personalities were pilloried unmercifully and many a public façade crumbled under the impact.

All of this was good for The Beatles and their successors because it meant that their irreverence and easy non-conformism, while shocking some, was welcomed gladly by others, quite apart from their younger audience.

Pop Art was also breaking into the scene at the beginning of the decade. Young painters were busy making colossal 'idols' of the crass, insignificant items of mass production. They were concerned with the *immediate*, the *telling image*, much as the new TV producers and film-makers were.

All told, there seemed to be a concerted effort to prod Britain awake, to make her question long-accepted beliefs and prejudices. Once more The Beatles, if a little less knowing and sophisticated than those intellectuals of the media might like, fitted happily into the atmosphere of challenge.

Asking questions is normally a healthy habit, and a good

deal of this refreshing debate was long overdue. But already there were signs of a preoccupation with questions rather than answers, with destruction rather than creation.

The attack on existing values, like that of the Rock 'n' Roll generation, arose indirectly from an agnostic position. If a good God couldn't be reckoned on, then everything anyone believed was open to question. But belief in nothing wasn't the only consequence of this period of enquiry.

Chesterton once said that: 'When people cease to believe in God, they do not believe in nothing, but anything.' Bernard Levin called the sixties a 'credulous age'. It was a period of gullibility and gurus, from John F. Kennedy through Martin Luther King to the Maharishi and Timothy Leary. There were takers for them all. Some believe it was a period of great optimism and faith. I see it as a desperate search for certainty.

That was undoubtedly the case as far as The Beatles were concerned. Their audience demanded from them a leadership and quality of life that would give them something tangible to refer to. They wanted guidance, however limited, even if it was about looks. The Beatles, perhaps unconsciously, accepted the role. And according to John Lennon they became 'more popular than Jesus Christ'.

The Beatles

It was a controversial statement at the time. Both the press and the church mistook it for a blasphemy. As it happened, it was a pretty bald statement of fact. They *were* more popular than Christ among teenagers. The church and the storybooks, in lethal combination with the rationalism of the scientists and philosophers, had seen to that. To the youth of the sixties, Jesus appeared a friendly but flower-picking moral teacher who was horribly murdered by power-crazy Romans.

The Beatles
'Played the amiable, local-lads-made-good game to the limit, but at the same time remained aloof from the milling throng'

Apart from highlighting the fact that Britain was no longer the Christian country it claimed to be, John Lennon's statement witnessed to the demand of The Beatles' audiences for contemporary heroes. There was at the time a hero famine. John F. Kennedy came pretty close, but he died the year The Beatles arrived. Martin Luther King was around, but he only served a sectional interest-group of youth and his time was yet to come. In the early sixties there was no one.

In any case, the old-style heroes weren't believable. They didn't fit into the social and ideological framework of the sixties. The Beatles did. The climate was exactly right for young, unrespectable working-class heroes.

The Beatles were not in fact very working class—but they fitted everyone's image, so it didn't matter. They were much more fun than the hero of *Look Back in Anger*. They were witty, ironic and sharp. They gave the press as good as they got and despite the constant scrum of reporters and photographers that surged around them, they remained somehow untouched. They caricatured their own scouse accents and played the amiable, local-lads-made-good game to the limit. But at the same time they remained aloof from the milling throng. All the time, they had a kind of four-man private joke going on which no one else could penetrate. They had a magical ability to seem accessible but remain inviolate. It was something that gave The Beatles a special quality, that enabled their fans to identify with them completely and to worship them.

The Beatles seldom took a committed stand on any issue; they never pronounced against the government or the church; they just flicked them aside as if they were of only passing interest. They made everything revolve around themselves. They were a unique phenomenon and they revolutionized Pop. Other artists have sold more records and earned more money, yet none have caused such an explosion. Once The Beatles had appeared it seemed impossible to understand what life had been without them.

The Beatles' music was new and exciting. Early numbers were raucous and a bit clumsy, and their first few singles, though magical in their simplicity and charm, were hardly earth-shattering. Despite that, 'Love me do' and 'Please please me' were fresh and lively enough to win over their audience.

Lennon and McCartney's song-writing was improving all the time. By 1964 The Beatles' songs were beginning to reflect much more clearly the characteristics that made them so appealing as personalities. They had the sparkle, the wit, the gentle curl-of-the-lip, the assurance—everything. The Beatles' music was an extension of their attitude to what was going on around them. That was something which had been missing since the heyday of Rock 'n' Roll.

The Beatles fulfilled a two-fold role. They reinforced the differences between the generations, being held up as objects of derision by the one and of admiration by the other: 'If you grow your hair any longer you're gonna look like one of those Beatles!' What finer accolade could there be?

At the same time the older generation was beginning to look to The Beatles for some sort of explanation as to why young people were as they were. The media had never really been interested in Elvis's opinions; they weren't sure he really had any. But The Beatles were much sharper; they gave the impression of having all the answers. Consequently their opinions, worthwhile or not, were sought on every matter. The Beatles played polite games with the mediamen. Their answers were uncommitted.

The Beatles' audience widened: Rock 'n' Roll had appealed largely to a working-class audience. Middle-class reserve and 'good taste' had formed a fragile barrier against the rudimentary and aggressive qualities of Rock. The melody of The Beatles' songs and their obvious wit and intelligence won the middle-class teenagers over.

American teenagers seemed to give The Beatles a much more revolutionary role than the British, seeing them as their spokesmen. It was a new role for Rock music. With Elvis it was his pose and looks that fans responded to, but with The Beatles it went further. Their image and their clothes were imitated, but it was their irreverence that caught the imagination of young people.

The Beatles pushed adult politics and the games of the rich out of the news. Suddenly the heroes and the music of the young were the subject of public debate. The attention focussed on The Beatles' clothes and hair made everyone more conscious of what other young people wore. Long hair had been considered shocking, but The Beatles were breaking down these barriers. Their long hair, like everything else, became a matter of discussion. When sons horrified their parents by growing their own hair, it was a gesture of defiance, a blow for freedom in solidarity with the group. The older generation at that time thought The Beatles were the ultimate in decadence. But they hadn't met The Rolling Stones.

The Rolling Stones

The Rolling Stones were from the start aggressive, intolerant and impatient with convention. Everything about The Stones was calculated to shock. The Beatles' hair had been shaggy, but theirs was *disgusting* by the standards of the day. The Beatles had only one potentially nasty character: John Lennon. *All* of The Stones were nasty. Two shadowy figures, Bill Wyman and Charlie Watts, lurked silent and menacing in the background. The three front men seemed positively bizarre.

Mick Jagger looked like an effeminate hoodlum. On stage he chicken-strutted, wriggled his hips and contorted his face, using his prominent lips as an extra stage prop. He out-Elvised Elvis and scared the nation's mothers half to death. Keith Richard looked more like a borstal boy than the ex-art student he was. He slung his guitar down low and oozed menace. Brian Jones on the other hand was beautiful. He had long straight golden hair and well-modelled features. Yet there was a tired decadence about his good looks.

The Stones behaved as badly as they looked. They were rude to press and public alike and lounged in delinquent poses for the photographers. And there was the famous night when three of them urinated against a petrol station wall in West Ham, London. They were fined £5. Valuable publicity has seldom cost so little.

The Stones caught the prevailing mood of defiance. Young people were gaining in confidence step by step. Through the public life of The Stones, they were beginning to see how far they could push the older generation. The Stones were like medieval champions fighting on behalf of peasants. Fans were quite prepared to look on and cheer. But the fact that The Stones and The Beatles were there meant that teenagers were braver in their defiance of convention. During the mid-sixties more and more boys flouted school rules by growing their hair over the collar. It was a small but significant gesture of defiance and antipathy between pupils and teachers worsened.

The Beatles showed a great deal of interest in their appearance. The Stones, too, had very definite tastes in clothes—though less neat and less consistent than The Beatles. Clothes assumed an Italian look. Shoes were pointed or chiselled, trousers tight and narrow without turn-ups, jackets had thin lapels or no lapels at all, and shirt collars were often buttoned down, tabbed or pinned. The style stood out against the comfortable baggy dress of the older generation.

The Rolling Stones
'Brought upon themselves more scorn and adult hysteria than any musicians before or since. For the most part they enjoyed it'

The young were asserting themselves, defining their own sense of taste and style over and against that of their parents. Those who had become so disillusioned with the conventional catalogue of ideals, beliefs and lifestyles were beginning to find an identity.

The Stones' music was as tough and uncompromising as their public image. Because of their more obviously rebellious qualities they lasted longer as symbols of defiance. The Beatles had a certain charm which, while it ensured their success, also made them vulnerable to the affection of older people. The more dissident young didn't like this and their belief in the Stones as the spear-head of the teenage attack was strengthened.

It's difficult to exaggerate the impact of The Rolling Stones. They brought upon themselves more scorn and adult hysteria than any musicians before or since. For the most part they enjoyed it. Often they courted derision because it placed them outside petty convention and more firmly in the role of folk heroes. They were outlaws.

Nasty music

The nastiness of the Stones was understandable, perhaps even honest; but their wanton destructiveness was not healthy. It showed a desire to break with unwanted tradition—but without alternatives. Once again the word 'freedom' played a big part. The Stones were battling for a selfish freedom, a liberty with no strings attached. But destruction was only a part of their music.

Compare the two songs, 'Satisfaction' and 'Sympathy for the devil'. Both are classic Stones' songs and neither of them are in any sense romantic, but there is a difference in the underlying mentality that produced them. 'Satisfaction' isn't a tremendously uplifting number in the moral sense, but it has a basic honesty. 'I can't get no satisfaction' doesn't look for satisfaction beyond appetite. But everyone feels a sense of hopelessness and unrealized desire at some time or another. It's normal.

By contrast, 'Sympathy for the devil' is a deliberate projection into the world of evil. It is an immensely strong piece of music, probably one of The Stones most accomplished works, but it is the product of a disordered mind. The song has an inverted perspective on reality. The world is seen through the devil's eyes and is therefore centred on and determined by him. The whole concept of sympathy for the devil reverses the meaning of good and evil. It is completely destructive. The song betrays an interest in evil for evil's sake which, despite protests to the contrary, can never be an innocent indulgence.

Ever since its beginning Rock 'n' Roll had been accused of being an agent for evil. The accusation has recurred over the years. In America much of it had to do with the white distrust for anything that came out of the black culture. Much was made of the African roots of the music. Older whites felt that Rock was basically primitive and erotic. It was the rhythm that worried them most. It was well known that tribal dances were liable to induce a trance, and also that many of the dances (fertility and war dances), were sexually or aggressively motivated.

African music and Rock do not inevitably tread the same path. African music was an integral part of religion, ritual and tribal hierarchy. To dance was to worship, and the trance—if a witch-doctor or a dancer pushed himself that far—was part of the worship, not a blind product of the music.

Rock is neither tribal or religious. The focus is on excitement, a release from boredom. Admittedly it has always been a physical music, yet there has always been a *conscious* edge to Rock. Because it has lacked the dimension of worship, the pressure on dancers to let go of themselves, to empty themselves for a spirit to enter, has not been the same.

Rock is not inherently evil. Some of it has been distasteful. But there has always been a close alliance between the music, mentality and lifestyle. A change in mentality inevitably affects the music and the lifestyle. Neither can remain static.

Merseysound and R & B

There was some other good music in the early to mid-sixties but it never carried the image and influence of The Beatles and The Stones.

In Britain, the Merseysound was foisted on the public by the music business. It was a typical manoeuvre. Instead of looking for groups with the same personal and musical qualities as The Beatles, they went for scouse accents and Beat groups. As a result they made a packet and helped form the distinctive British Beat-group sound of the next few years.

More significant, musically, were the British R & B groups who, rather than following the surface sound of The Beatles, were inspired by the same roots. Groups like The Animals, The Yardbirds, The Kinks, Manfred Mann and The Spencer Davis Group adopted a less frothy, more gutsy style. It provided a stronger musical base for future developments. Individuals in those groups came to the fore in the late sixties when musicians' abilities and intelligence were taken more seriously.

Eric Clapton, Jeff Beck (eventually a guitar hero in his own right) and Jimmy Page (later of Led Zeppelin) had all played with The Yardbirds. Eric Burdon came from The Animals. Ray Davies remained with The Kinks, but his songs developed enormously. With few exceptions the Merseysound and its counterparts—The Merseybeats, Billy J. Kramer and the Dakotas, The Searchers, The Dave Clark Five, Brian Poole and the Tremeloes—did not.

Suddenly, after the lull of the early sixties, everything was happening. In Britain, Beat groups seemed to sprout from every nook and cranny. During the early years of The Beatles, there were estimated to be over 100 Beat groups in the Liverpool area alone, and something like 1,000 all told over the country from 1960 to 1966. That doesn't include the hundreds of groups constantly forming, breaking up and re-grouping without ever playing to the public, or maybe playing a social or a youth club and no more. Schoolkids and factory workers, clerks and labourers, all wanted to get in on the action. Music had once more become the life of youth.

It wasn't the songs that were important. It was the glamour, the knowledge that to be in a group was to be *someone*, even if you only strummed the three basic chords. It was so easy to feel lost and unimportant in school, industry and bureaucracy. Being part of a Beat group, or even simply collecting records, gave teenagers a place, something which defined their tastes and their interests. Perhaps more important, it declared them young. Pop wasn't for anyone else. It was part of a collective, private understanding. Again this was an important part of the search to be at home in the world.

Beat groups weren't alone in the music world. The mid-sixties saw a bevy of white girl singers on both sides of the Atlantic. Most of them sang the songs they were given with varying degrees of style. Only Brenda Lee, and maybe Dusty Springfield, stood out as having any real oomph. For the rest, it was, in traditional terms, a man's game.

Stateside

When the Beatles came (leaving the door open for The Rolling Stones) the youth of America claimed them immediately as their champions. They took them much more seriously than the British did, because they seemed to see them much more clearly as revolutionary figures.

The delight with which American kids met the Beatles spilled over to other British artists. The kids were not all that choosy. Along with the better groups, they took on the garbage as well. Even groups like Herman's Hermits and The Dave Clark Five, seen by most people in Britain as schmucks from the very beginning, found themselves unbelievably successful in the States.

At the same time America was making a musical response of her own. For a long while black musicians had been stirring a new mixture in their cauldron. It was called Soul.

Black artists had a great heritage to plunder. They didn't have to borrow, as white musicians did. They just dipped into their own culture. Soul was a combination of Gospel and R & B. It had the passion of the one and the rhythm of the other. The black people of America were going through their own development and the black church was losing its grip on young people. This new generation was beginning to jib at the years of oppression their race had been forced to suffer. Many felt that the church had simply accepted it as the cross it had to bear. Some black singers were beginning to realize they could win a kind of acceptability among the white population through music. It was an imperfect arrangement, but one they were willing to take.

Most black artists of the sixties were raised among church communities, and Gospel was their music. It was an almost instinctive reaction for them to mix this music with R & B—the music their church leaders had warned them to avoid. So Soul emerged. Its early exponents were Ray Charles, James Brown and Sam Cooke. These were shortly followed by the Tamla Motown artists, the most famous being The Supremes, The Temptations and Stevie Wonder. Then there were the Stax/Volt/Atlantic stable, including Wilson Pickett, Otis Redding and Arthur Conley.

In another camp, Phil Spector had been producing his own minor masterpieces for several years before The Beatles arrived, with girl groups like The Crystals and The Ronettes. Overshadowed for a while by the British invasion, he left his final works of genius for a last ditch stand, with 'You've lost that lovin' feeling' by The Righteous Brothers and 'River deep mountain high' by Ike and Tina Turner. He is remembered more than the artists because he was the creator of both pieces of music. He was the first producer to become a star in his own right. Both records are outstanding, both as far as his own work is concerned and the history of Pop.

Who else is there to pick out from the American catalogue of post-Beatles pop? The Four Seasons, perhaps—with Frankie Valli's falsetto voice soaring over the treble back-up singing packaged teenage mythology: 'Sherry', 'Big girls don't cry' and 'Walk like a man'. They all have that strange quality which brings memories of the sixties flooding back.

The surfing sound came and went. It was formed around the teenage sub-culture on the wide sandy beaches of California. The early Beach Boys' music best captured the essence of it. Brian Wilson's songs evoked images of long, carefree summers; of coasting in hotted-up autos ('I get around' and 'Little deuce coupé'); surfing ('surfing USA' and 'surfin' safari'); of girls ('California girls'). To listen to the songs, life seems all 'Dance dance dance' and 'Fun fun fun'. Once again youth was the hero, this time bronzed, blonde and free to live totally without restrictions until September. From the grubby streets of Hounslow, where I lived, it made California seem a paradise.

Tamla Motown was churning out hits, managing records of rare wonder, but getting more predictable with every record. Herb Alpert and his Tijuana Brass crept in somewhere, and sold a lot of records, but that seemed to be the limit of the initial response to The Beatles. The real response was on its way, and it was Protest. In 1968 Barry McGuire had a hit with 'Eve of Destruction'. Peter, Paul and

Mary had had an even earlier hit with Bob Dylan's 'Blowin' in the wind'. They were indicators of a new kind of unrest and a new kind of music.

The Mods

Meanwhile in Britain a youthful pursuit of pleasure as the chief good emerged and it soon found a creed and a liturgy in the form of the Mods.

Like the Teds, the Mods developed in London streets. They were mostly the children of working-class or lower middle-class families. They were dedicated to three things: clothes, music and youth. Legend has it they spent half of each week's wages on what they wore. They also developed a fierce partisan feeling for their music (Soul, and white R & B). They lived in the belief that to be old was to be beyond hope. To be young and live a life of youthful abandonment was the only thing for it in a fairly hopeless world.

The Mods weren't a surprise manifestation that happened without warning. Their attitudes and way of life were very much an extension of what had been happening during the early part of the sixties.

The arch Mods were a fairly select group, but their influence swept Britain. They were the first largely working-class group who consciously and consistently tried to live out their own alternative principles.

Pete Meaden was the arch Mod. He was the original manager of The Who (then The High Numbers) who were themselves the arch Mod Pop group. He said that 'Mod' was: 'a society unto itself . . . you have your own values, your own set of time scales, your own units of existence which is to have a good time.'

Because of work or school, the Mod life took place at weekends or in the evenings. Pete Meaden, admittedly a unique example, would spend literally the *whole* weekend on 'the life'. He would: 'hit out on Friday night, high on speed, down to "Ready, Steady, Go" (a live TV Pop programme), down to the Scene Club, dance all night till Saturday morning. Saturday you'd go shopping, to buy a pullover, a scarf or something—pair of socks 'cos you feet hurt dancing all night in desert boots, and then all through Saturday night again at the Scene Club all through to Sunday morning. That's when the come down comes on, 'cos you can't sustain it much more . . . and you start heading home to Mama's place.'

Work was a necessary drudge. There was no virtue or future in it. But when the real life started at night, Mods wanted to be more awake than usual. And that's where the pep pills came in. Amphetamines were as central to Mod life as music and dancing. The energy-burn necessary for a weekend like that just wasn't possible without them. Mods would ignore the blisters they left on their tongues in order to extend 'the life'. They felt they had to grasp every available opportunity with both hands, since the working week took such a large chunk from their real lives.

Mods kept a fairly low profile during the day. Those at school wore their uniforms with distaste, though they might get away with a button-down shirt or good shoes. At work they adopted an even more low-key approach. As often as not they were the filing-clerks, the messenger-boys of the vast city bureaucracy. They formed an organic underground, accepting the boredom of the work for the sake of the money.

Getting adults 'on your own ground' was an important development in the generation-war. As Pete Townshend of The Who said: 'It was acceptable, this was important, their way of dressing was hip, it was fashionable, it was clean and it was groovy. You could be a bank clerk, man, it was acceptable. You got them on your own ground. They thought, "well, there's a smart young lad" . . . you didn't get people uptight.'

There was an implicit self-confidence in the Mod movement. Mods were subtle and devious. Instead of showing their scorn for the world of parents, teachers and employers by deliberate provocation, Mods parodied the dress of the older generation. They had suits, shirts and ties. But they were suits tailored to individual requirements, expensive shirts in polka dots, and wild ties.

They didn't fight the old men, they turned their backs on them, and let them think what they wanted. It was by far the most stylish revolt of all. Their image and cool were the supreme virtues.

Their style wasn't appreciated by everyone. As the Mod movement spread out of London it became mobile. Suddenly high streets up and down the land echoed to the staccato sound of motor scooters.

Inevitably, a rivalry developed between Mods and Rockers. Rockers were the leather jacket, motor cycle brigade. Up to this point they had rightly considered themselves kings of the road. Imagine their chagrin when the roads suddenly became infested with these pop-popping little insects sporting (as was the Mod habit) twenty mirrors apiece, myriad non-functional headlamps and an optional foxtail. They were like motor cycles in drag. And the Rockers reacted with the self-righteousness of generations of queer-bashers.

Mods returned their hostility and there were several pitched battles at south-coast seaside resorts. However, gang tactics were not their aim. Individualism was. Although their clothes conformed to a pattern, their privacy, especially on the dance floor, was sacred. They were all the same, but different. Pete Meaden said the individuality was: '. . . a style of your own, so succinctly beautiful and self contained, where privacy was everything because you were all the same.'

Girls had to take second place. It was the boys who set the

pace. And it appears that all-night dancing and amphetamines don't exactly do wonders for a chap's sex drive.

In the wake of The Beatles and The Stones, a third generation became interested in R & B. In 1965 and 1966 there were spotty, adolescent R & B groups shooting up everywhere. Most of these young bands thought they could cope with R & B but they left Soul well alone. That was a black preserve. But Mods adopted Soul as their music. Percy Sledge, Arthur Conley and James Brown became the heroes. So were the Tamla artists.

Music was of the utmost importance to Mods. As a group they were committed to youth. Mods mostly met in clubs where there was either live or recorded music. If they hung around coffee bars, then the juke boxes were there; and there were always the pirate radio stations beaming 24-hour music. They could surround themselves with music at any time.

The Who

The Mods had no leaders but they did have heroes. The boss heroes were The Who. Mods accepted them because the group's songs released many of their aggressions, tensions and frustrations.

Pete Townshend, guitarist and mastermind of The Who, created a small revolution in Pop by moving away from the love song as his main vehicle. The Who's second hit, called 'Anyway, anywhere, anyhow', was a stubborn declaration of freedom and of scorn for the established things. Lines like:

> 'I can do anything, talk anyhow . . .
> Nothing gets in my way not even locked doors
> Don't follow any lines, that've been laid before'

were very close to the Mod idea. Then The Who managed to pull a Mod anthem out of the bag. 'My generation' was a

The Who
'Mods accepted them because the group's songs released many of their aggressions, tensions and frustrations'

heavy put-down of all things old and an assertion of youth supremacy. With a perfect touch, Roger Daltrey, The Who's lead singer, sang with a menacing stutter:

> 'People try to put us down
> Just because we get around
> Things they do look awful c-c-cold
> I hope I die before I get old.'

It was no great poetry. It was simply the voice of someone who felt his generation had been pushed around and wanted to push back. The Who certainly gave every indication of that in their stage performances. With Pete Townshend crashing huge chords after leaping high in the air and then grinding out violent feedback off his guitar, Roger Daltrey swinging his mike round his head like a lariat and Keith Moon kicking his drums over at the end of a set, their act was not short on aggression.

Mod peters out

Free living is difficult to keep up and Mod was a movement of such high energy that it could not be sustained for long. It had no answers to the bigger questions about values or about where life really was going, and it petered out.

The sixties was not a period famous for its solutions, it was known better for its questions and theories. Mod wasn't a theory, but it was an attempt to live in a different way from the norm. Symptoms from the mid-fifties showed themselves again during this time. They were the signs of a generation trying to come to terms with a world without norms, without rules and without love. A world without God.

For the Mods, to believe in self, your mates and the good-time was sufficient. It took them out of a drab world into a new reality. With a pocketful of Frenchies or purple hearts they could sustain a sleepless madcap weekend until Sunday morning. But always, when the peaky come-down arrived on Sunday morning, on the tube to mama's place, the world seemed too real. It was a brave attempt at 'the life', the first for a Rock 'n' Roll generation. But it remained a negative movement. The search for freedom continued.

3
Trouble in the Boulevard
(1960-66)

Teddy boys provided a caricature of the fifties. By the mid-sixties they had been shaken from the top spot by two new types. There was the fashionable kid following the wake of The Beatles and The Stones, with a transistor grafted to his ear. And there was the scruffy anti-establishment beatnik.

As the fifties faded and the sixties said hallo, many of the young population, particularly in America, began to be aware of the political and social situation in their country. And they were bold enough to go a step further than the generation before them. They protested that the culture they had inherited was not only dull, inhibiting and hypocritical, it was also in some respects wrong.

A generation committed to fending off sermons and criticisms from its elders was ready to preach back. They challenged their parents' whole moral stand-point and then adopted a new one of their own.

They were not objecting to the ideals their parents laid claim to—peace, freedom, justice and equality. What troubled them was the glaring truth that these great principles were nowhere in evidence in the institutions, homes and everyday lives of people in America and Britain. These values were being compromised and rendered meaningless in the interests of money, power and progress.

Generations of cynics had seen the same thing. This time, however, it sparked off enough anger and conscience to mobilize youth in great numbers. This was seen in the Civil Rights Movement and the anti-Vietnam demonstrations. The new movement gave kids a cause to identify with. They discovered a set of ideals they could make their own. They leapt in, firing moral salvoes against government corruption. They genuinely believed they could call the world to order, that by appealing to reason and conscience they could make men free.

The Civil Rights Movement sprang particularly out of a need to fight racial discrimination in the USA. The coloured population in Montgomery, Alabama, formed a united front under the leadership of Dr Martin Luther King and in 1960 boycotted the city's bus service which operated a segregated seating policy. King's leadership not only unified the blacks but also prompted the consciences of many white liberals and radicals, encouraging them to become involved. The Montgomery boycott and other demonstrations attracted progressively more attention and provoked a great surge of support from the young. The new wave of political interest was evident in the predominantly white student organizations formed in the early sixties, for instance the Student Non-violent Co-ordinating Committee and Students for a Democratic Society. At this stage, as the title SNCC suggests, protests were committed to non-violence, with just a hint of civil disobedience.

Black organizations, such as the old-established Congress of Racial Equality and the National Association for the Advancement of Colored Peoples, co-ordinated the efforts of various groups and individuals in wave after wave of public protest against discriminatory laws. This provided youth with a role and a romantic lifestyle. They were no longer spotty teenagers with breath problems. They were crusaders with the light of battle in their eyes and a stirring marching song on their lips.

Folk and Protest

It was partly the romance of protest, but also genuine anger at injustice, that focussed the attentions of young people on the plight of the underprivileged. Many of those involved in the Civil Rights Movement, either actively or as sympathetic spectators, came from fairly middle-class backgrounds. In reaction against this they temporarily turned their backs on Pop which at the time was going through its thinnest patch: shallow and commercial; post-Rock 'n' Roll but pre-Beatles. They turned instead to Folk music. It was, they thought, an art-form 'of the people'—the real home-made genuine article.

Folk had a long tradition of topical story-telling, of championing the oppressed and narrating the exploits of local or national heroes. It was a natural for the protest generation. Their interest in the Folk tradition extended to Blues, taking in the songs of the very people they were fighting for.

A strong and growing minority interest in Folk already existed in Britain and the States. Many of its exponents, if not politically active, were politically aware or committed. This new interest swelled the ranks considerably, creating an enormous Folk boom which spread to a wide audience through the media.

Many of the gaggle of Folk singers who sprang up in the sixties looked back to the depressed years of the thirties for inspiration. Most of all they looked back to Woody Guthrie, the grandaddy and senior Folk hero of the protest movement. His influence was all too visible in the content of the songs and in the lifestyle of the musicians. He was so much what every young Folk-singer wanted to be.

Woody Guthrie hoboed round America, hitching rides, jumping boxcars, with nothing but a guitar and a head full of songs and stories. Everywhere he went he took the part of the poorly paid, the ill-used and the uncared for. He joined picket-lines and sang to strike-meetings. He sang to students, telling them what was happening to poor whites and blacks in the mines and the Californian orchards. Musically he brought a fresh adaptation of the story-telling ballad style from Anglo/American Country songs and talking Blues, plus telling, ironic pay-off lines from the black Blues tradition. It was this wit and cleverness with words, combined with the hobo/radical/guitar-player image, that most influenced the heroes of the sixties—among them Bob Dylan.

Peter Seeger and Odeta and other, lesser, lights kept topical Protest-song alive between the time of Guthrie and the later Folk boom. They, too, were zealous in highlighting America's social and military sins. They were the Mummy and Daddy of the Folk singers who came from all over the States and ghettoed themselves in towns like Cambridge and Boston and, inevitably, in New York's hobo paradise, Greenwich Village.

Innumerable song-writers and singers made up the Folk coterie in Greenwich Village. They were roughly in two camps—the purists and the interpreters/songwriters.

Purists were musicians dominated by an obsessive enthusiasm for the authentic. Their renditions were attempts at carbon-copying original traditional material.

The second group, including Bob Dylan, approached traditional songs with a 'loose and goosey' attitude. They plundered Negro Blues and Spirituals or white Country songs. They sang them in their own way, trying different arrangements or putting them to new tunes. They gave old songs new life. A good example is Bob Dylan's first album,

Bob Dylan. Many others in this group wrote their own songs, a growing proportion of them protesting against war, poverty and racialism.

In order to encourage the writing of Protest songs a paper called *Broadside* began publication early in 1962. It set out to publish Protest songs as they were written, so that singers, amateur and professional alike, could have access to new numbers. Folk singers and the Civil Rights Movement were moving along the same path, deploying their forces and organizing their weaponry.

Most Protest songs written in this period were awful. The writers stumbled on a problem common to all artists with a burning message to communicate. They tend to concentrate on the message and let the form they're using go hang. So most Protest song-writers concentrated first on getting the message right then on making it rhyme, and lastly on fitting a tune to it. Only in the first flush of collective idealism, in the heady atmosphere of a thousand-strong marching choir, or the self-congratulatory atmosphere of a concert by a Joan Baez or a Pete Seeger did the songs gather any power.

The fact that singers were prepared to write and sing songs about freedom and justice did, if only to a limited degree, bring these big and important issues into public debate. The songs began to gain popularity outside the minority folk-buff circles, in the mainstream of Civil Rights marchers and sympathizers. Soon they were put on record, and songs such as 'If I had a hammer' and 'Blowin' in the wind' began to be played on the radio. The media pundits had a time and a half exploring the depths of these new, meaningful songs. Meanwhile adults, young workers and school kids argued the toss for and against the bomb. So even the crop of bogus opportunistic 'Protest' songs, such as Jonathan King's dreadful 'It's good news week . . . someone's dropped a bomb somewhere contaminating the atmosphere and blackening the sky' helped make these controversies a public issue.

The Protest song movement showed clearly for the first time that values and ideas could be communicated powerfully and explicitly through the music, via the media. It's comparatively rare for music, or any kind of art form as committed and preachy as Protest, to be given so much exposure. Despite its earnestness, and in stark contrast to the everyday froth of much of the Pop music surrounding it, it soon became a craze. Not everybody who bought Barry McGuire's 'Eve of destruction' turned into a card-holding member of the Civil Rights Movement or the Campaign for Nuclear Disarmament despite the call to:

'Think of all the hate there is in Red China
Then take a look around to Selma, Alabama . . .
And you tell me, over and over again, my friend,
Ah, you don't believe we're on the eve of destruction.'

Not only did the Protest song explosion show the potential of Pop music to express ideas and values, and the power of the media in helping to punch the message home, but it helped give the Civil Rights Movement a united front. It was stirring to sing 'Blowin' in the wind' or 'We shall overcome' either in small groups, or on the march. It gave a sense of united purpose against a common enemy. And with so much idealism tied to an uncertain hope, great reserves of morale were essential.

Bob Dylan

The three great phenomena of Pop in the sixties were The Beatles, The Rolling Stones and Bob Dylan.

Dylan appeared in New York in 1961 and in a very short time, helped by people like Joan Baez, Columbia's John Hammond and manager Albert Grossman, reached outside the tight-knit Greenwich Village Folk circle to become the

Bob Dylan
'He made it the thing to be earnest and "cool" to be a cynic.... He became a prophet'

premier poet of the Civil Rights Movement. Soon he was an international star. He began by re-interpreting old Blues and old Folk tunes. But he soon showed a distinctive and unusual songwriting talent.

Dylan's Protest songs were of a much higher quality than any of his contemporaries'. Woodie Guthrie had been his hero, too. But apart from the occasional plagiarism Dylan leant on him lightly.

Dylan's second album, *The freewheelin' Bob Dylan*, which came out in May 1963, had all the ingredients the young Folkies, students, and would-be radicals could wish for. It had hard, uncompromising Protest songs: 'Blowin' in the wind', 'Hard rain's a-gonna fall', 'Oxford town'. There was sharp wit and crazy humour: 'Talking World War II Blues' and 'Honey just allow me one more chance'. And there were bitter-sweet songs of romance: 'Girl from the north country' and, 'Don't think twice, it's all right'. To round it all off he had the ideal image photo on the record sleeve—Bob Dylan and his girl walking arm-in-arm down a snowy New York street, looking very Bohemian and freewheelin'. The album sleeve and the songs inside managed to capture the feel, the image, and lifestyle that so many kids in the early sixties were aiming for.

Richard Farina, author of the classic underground novel *Been down so-long it looks up to me*, said at the time: 'Behind the college students of America today, no matter what their protest against segregation, injustice and thermo-nuclear war, are the realities of their parents, the monthly cheque and their home town. *The freewheelin' Bob Dylan* as the title of his album sets him up, lives in a world that is the realm of their alter ego.'

It was true. I acted out my own Bob Dylan fantasies in the same way. He made it the thing to be earnest, and 'cool' to be a cynic. Had he been an ageing professor, it wouldn't have worked. I used to walk around the streets of Hounslow in winter, freezing to death in only a jacket, because Dylan didn't wear one on the cover. The thing that was missing was the girl—I had to imagine her. But I felt heroic all the same.

Dylan's fans began to invest his words with much significance. He became a prophet. His interviews showed him to be aloof, ironical and cunning with words. The Civil Rights Movement adopted him as their resident poet. His role was confirmed when he appeared at the Newport Folk Festival in 1963. Throughout the weekend, singer after singer paid tribute to him by singing his compositions. Dylan's own performance was the climax of the proceedings. The whole festival was marked by the constant pressure of political and social realities outside. There was a feeling of being part of a movement. Dylan, to everyone's mind, was one of the leaders.

He cherished his 'freewheelin'' life as much as his fans aspired to it. The amount of faith and responsibility that was heaped on him, however, soon became a burden: he was trapped beneath it. In his role as spokesman for the disaffiliated young he attracted many to the cause. Inevitably, though, as he became more popular, many of his followers paid lip-service to his ideas simply because it was fashionable.

For all that, Dylan was the first major Pop-figure to change people's ideas in Britain and America. Young people wanted to say hard, biting things about the society they felt so bitter about. They didn't have the words. Bob Dylan did. He spoke for them. Kids wanted to have free, independent, exciting lives. But they weren't convinced or courageous enough to do so. Bob Dylan lived for them. Dylan's audience absorbed his opinions and perceptions and made them their own. No one had really done that before. No one else really tried to talk with any clarity before. Dylan revealed a social consciousness and uncompromising intelligence, all of which came through in songs like 'Hard rain's a-gonna fall'.

> 'I met a white man who walked a black dog . . .
> I met a young woman whose body was burning
> I met a young girl she gave a me a rainbow
> I met one man who was wounded in love
> I met another man who was wounded with hatred
> And it's a hard, it's a hard, it's a hard
> It's a hard rain's gonna fall.'

Dylan piles up almost random thoughts and perceptions, giving a strong vision of a threatened world. He wrote this song during the Cuban missile crisis. It was a personal song but one with which his audience felt immediate sympathy. That was what they needed, someone with fresh insight to see for them. Bob Dylan was talented and original enough to do it.

Dylan's individual vision and his skilful knife-play with words impressed both the record-buying public and other musicians—not just the Folk singers.

This is why all Pop and Rock of the late sixties was 'post-Dylan'. He revolutionized the Pop scene. By the end of 1964 he'd recorded two more albums, *Times they are a-changing* and *Another side of Bob Dylan*. With a slowly shifting emphasis they contained much the same ingredients as *the freewheelin' Bob Dylan*; Protest songs, fun songs, love songs and personal songs about the past or about things he saw around him, like 'Bob Dylan's Dream':

> 'As easy it was to tell black from white
> it was all that easy to tell wrong from right
> and our choices were few and the thoughts never hit
> that the one road we travelled would ever shatter or split'.

Dylan's open and unique way of writing encouraged many others to attempt a more serious approach. For many of them—The Beatles, for instance—song-writing had been a matter of writing hit singles. It needed someone to make the break—then The Beatles, The Stones and many others felt they could use images in their songs that had previously been the poets' preserve. The band-wagon jumpers were quick to see the commercial possibilities of pseudo-poetic lyrics and exploited them. Once more Jonathan King, the arch-British-bandwagon-jumper, was first in the queue with a smooth piece of evocative nonsense—'Everyone's gone to the moon'.

Nevertheless the new influence had a tremendously liberating effect on music, and it was very healthy for the industry. It brought a new audience.

Slowly, as the electric guitars and drums began to be used as backing for poetic or Protest lyrics, and as some of these crept into the charts, a large proportion of the Folk audience was won over. However, some thought that to use electricity was somehow to betray the pure Folk music heritage. Audiences booed Dylan the first time he used an electric band on stage. 'Judas' they called him. But only for a while.

Other musicians took up Dylan's poetry rather than his Protest. Over the years the romance of Protest faded for Dylan, too.

Punctured optimism

On 22 November 1963 American President, John F. Kennedy, was shot dead in Dallas, Texas. There is no computing the effects of his death. It made no immediate difference to the institutions or policies of America. But it hit hard and deep into the consciousnesses of millions of ordinary people around the globe. It cast a depressing gloom over the democratic West.

Many people in America and Britain felt that Kennedy had the sane, liberalizing influence needed to shake up the

American government and push through the reforms that groups such as the Civil Rights Movement asked for. His death punctured much of the optimism. Eric Andersen, a Folk singer and contemporary of Dylan, expressed in his own strange way what many people were feeling:

> 'Right after Kennedy, things started to get strange. The immunity that had been . . . Well, Folk music looked like it was going to be pretty heavy. Folk music had a medieval flair to it, and pageantry, it had a feeling of truth and of, yes we can do it, just freedom, and everybody's going to get it together and it is just going to be won. And Kennedy, he was sort of like the shadow of flight, he sort of protected this kind of thing. And then that bird got shot out of the sky and everybody was exposed, naked to all the frightening elements, the truth of the country. It had flown, that force had lost out. And people were depressed. The streets were very cold, man . . .'

The intelligent, middle-class young people—inspired by the cause of Civil Rights and stirred by the songs of Protest that surrounded them—were a romantic generation. Their ideals weren't based in any bedrock. They were a loosely held together hotch-potch of prejudices, hopes and assumptions: a variety of optimistic humanism, the feeling that man was basically good and if given the chance was capable of bettering himself. A single pin-prick was all that was needed to disperse these romanticized ideals. The assassination of President Kennedy was devastating. It shook everyone, but kids like this never stood a chance. I was only thirteen at the time, but it filled me with an unnameable horror. It was the first time the death of a public figure had really affected me. It was numbing.

Dylan had to play a concert the night after the assassination. He always opened his set with 'The times they are a-changin''. He said afterwards that he felt it was an impossible song to sing at that time. Its meaning had been destroyed. The times were changing but not for the better. Only the hard core of Civil Rights activists managed to hold on to their vision when faced with an event of this magnitude.

But Kennedy's death wasn't the only factor in the freedom marchers' loss of morale. Earlier in the year a black leader, Medgar Elvers, had been murdered only four days before President Kennedy was to present the Civil Rights bill before Congress. In September, two months before the assassination of the President, a bomb was thrown into a black church. Four little girls were killed. Kennedy's death seemed the final, intractable response of America to the cause of liberty.

Slowly it dawned on the reformers that the forces of reaction were so strong that a political patch-up job was not going to solve the problems. The de-segregation laws were being openly flouted by state governing bodies in the south. Grass-roots attitudes were not changing; the government wasn't changing. The H-bomb still cast its heavy shadow over world politics. Drastic action was called for if anything was going to happen.

This message was brought home more clearly by James Baldwin's book *The Fire Next Time* published in 1963. Baldwin, a black novelist and commentator prophesied the results of growing racial unrest in America. He caught the spirit that was flowing through young Americans, black and white. Compromise was impossible.

Vietnam then began to hit the headlines. Nothing could have been better calculated to push already frustrated young people into a more militant opposition to the government than to commit them to what they saw as a useless war.

Nineteen-sixty-five saw the speedy escalation of the war

TROUBLE IN THE BOULEVARD 65

and the equally speedy reaction of its opponents. At the beginning of the year, there were less than 20,000 American troops in Vietnam. By November there were almost 200,000. The same year saw the first suicide by fire on the Pentagon steps in an all-too-eloquent protest against the war. The first national anti-Vietnam war rally was also held.

Young men of draft age felt not only angry at the war, but threatened and enraged at the prospect of being forced to participate. It was a numbing thought to be asked to risk one's life in the service of a policy one thought was the product of gross immorality. It was no wonder that previously liberal, tolerant young people should turn to drastic measures to stop the war and to stop the government that perpetrated what they saw as madness. They knew that peaceful demonstration wasn't enough.

Vietnam became the focus of attention. The civil rights question might almost have been pushed into the background, except for the fact that the black community showed they had come to the same conclusions about their own situation. Hitting back was the answer. At the end of 1964 and into 1965 there were a series of riots in cities with large black populations.

This was the ferment that made the New Left. In Britain and Europe things were going the same way. The movement was dominated by the young. Their disgust was levelled not only at the forces of capitalism and imperialism but also at the liberals and the pacifists. The old left, the card-carrying communists were a target, too, accused of compromise, of theorizing, of selling out to the status quo. The New Left wanted revolution, bloody if necessary. They wanted a fresh start, an end to the fabric of society as it stood.

New directions

Dylan didn't turn militant when he grew disillusioned with the Protest movement. He turned in another direction. The change can be seen as early as 1964, a year before the Protest boom hit the British musical charts. That August he recorded an album called *Another side of Bob Dylan*.

Unlike his two previous albums, this contained no songs of explicit protest. The songs had moved into a kind of private, anarchic cynicism. Dylan had removed himself from the political arena. He was still singing songs about freedom but it was liberty of a different kind. 'The chimes of freedom' he sang about were:

> 'Tolling for the aching ones whose wounds cannot be nursed
> For the countless confused, accused, misused, strung-out ones and worse
> An' for every hung-up person in the whole wide universe
> An' we gazed upon the chimes of freedom flashing'.

It was not the freedom from home pressures that the fifties teenagers and the Pop generation of the sixties were after. Neither was it the Folk singers' freedom of the oppressed.

It was a private freedom: a freedom of *consciousness*. Dylan said to Phil Ochs, a Protest singer at that time: 'Politics is bullshit. It's all unreal. The only thing that's real is inside you. Your feelings.' This idea was suggesting itself to many as pacifism and non-violent protest waned. Dylan, true to his role, spoke these things first. It was the only strong alternative to militant action.

Dylan took Rock music into a new era. Impressed by Rock groups, especially The Beatles, he realized he needed to work with other musicians. For his fifth album, *Bringing it all back home*, he supported himself with a Rock backing. It was hardly heavy but it had a significant edge on his previous acoustic albums. Dylan's inner visions became progressively darker and more sinister. The songs were still angry, bitter and vengeful but now had no defined targets.

With this album Dylan really succeeded in combining the

cruel power of his lyrics with the most significant musical development of the twentieth century—Rock and Roll. He was shot-at by the Folk purists as well as the Folkie-radicals, both of whom felt betrayed.

Nevertheless, the great mass of Dylan fans were swept along with him. They liked his crazy humour and his manic nightmares, even if they didn't understand them. The fans, many of them weaned on Folk of the Protest era, followed Dylan into mainstream Rock. Their tastes imposed new demands on musicians and on the record industry. Like their fifties counterparts, they wanted music that was real to *their* everyday experience. They wanted idealism, commitment and poetry. They were better educated and more articulate than the Rockers. And they demanded a higher musical standard from their heroes.

Pop was still around, some of it good, some of it abysmal. It is ironic that Nancy Sinatra's dirge, 'These boots are made for walking' should hit number one in the States early in 1966, only a month after Simon and Garfunkel had been there with 'Sounds of silence'. In Britain 'Boots' was followed later in the year by The Stones' 'Paint it black' and The Beatles' 'Eleanor Rigby'—so music was looking up even if society wasn't.

In retrospect, Protest showed itself worthy but musically insufferable. Topical songs and propagandist songs inevitably lose their flavour out of their own time. These Protest songs were no different.

Despite the one-dimensional nature of Protest, it was a genuine voice. Not only did the generation stand on its hind legs to point out the evils of the world, it also made its contemporaries think about the issues. The protesters' aims were grand but they turned out to be dreams rather than real goals. The illusion of hope lasted only a few more years. Perhaps the real problem with the protest movement was its helpless self-righteousness.

As for the purists who gave Rock and Roll the cold shoulder, I think they should heed the words of Big Bill Broonzy, a thirties Blues singer: 'I guess all songs is Folk songs; I never heard no horse sing 'em.'

Ultimately the protest movement was the victim of its own idealism. It put so much faith in the ability of humanity to better itself that when humanity showed its real nature—selfish, bigoted, aggressive and cruel—there was no hope left. Some gave themselves up to cynicism. Others, embittered and desperate for a new world, prepared for attack. Yet more, without hope of peace in this world, looked for it within their own consciousness.

4
Summer in the City
(1966-69)

There was a smell of revolution in the air in the late sixties. It was not the usual revolutionary stench of cordite and explosives. It was a mixture of flowers, stink-bombs, marijuana, hot amplifiers and crowds. The title of The Lovin' Spoonful hit of 1966, 'Summer in the city', comes closest to the feel of the time. It was a period when everyone came out on the street to take the sun and relax. Yet it was imperfect, as summers always are in the city. To paraphrase the song, you couldn't help your neck getting dirty. You could never quite forget you were in a city.

The New Left were having another kind of urban summer. Neckties awry and sweat-stains round their armpits, they were busy in fraternity houses and in campus offices organizing the new society. Summer wasn't exactly fun for them but it was absorbing work. They had a vision.

By and large, conventional society couldn't see that something unusual was happening. Dylan had almost forecast the situation in his song of 1965, 'Ballad of a thin man':

'Something is happening here
But you don't know what it is
Do you, Mr Jones?'

An underground network was growing in Britain. Papers such as the *International Times* and *Oz* were set up. Release, a legal aid centre for people arrested on drugs charges was started. In America, Ken Kesey tripped out on acid and began persuading everyone else to do the same. The summer was coming.

The protest generation's inherent anti-establishment feeling remained, but it had shifted its ground. It was less prepared to bargain openly with adult society and was going underground.

There had been a distinct change in mental attitude. The Civil Rights Movement marchers saw themselves as an open challenge to the forces of government. It was their responsibility to launch an assault on the political conscience. But it didn't work. Slowly they came to the conclusion that they were faced with an administration with whom they could not reason on equal terms. They were up against an occupying power whose values clashed with theirs. And so the underground was born. Young people turned their backs on the establishment culture—gave it up as lost—and turned to their own generation for positive ideas and the hope of a new society.

This was reflected by a split in the world of Pop music. Pop, the daily top-forty musical diet, remained largely the same. It was still full of love and heartbreak, tender and true. It was more competently played and more intelligently handled than it had been. But the sentiments were the same, and so was its purpose. It was musical canteen fodder for the masses, colourfully packaged like canned goods, and just as tasteless.

On the other hand there was Rock. This was music that

took itself seriously—often too seriously. It attempted to become a conscious art-form where both music and words were important in themselves. Inevitably the distinctions between Rock and Pop were and are blurred because they so often blend into each other.

Pop

Pop audiences—the kind of people who listened to Sandie Shaw, Englebert Humperdink, The Monkees and the rest, and bought their records—had certain expectations. They simply wanted entertainment. The age-range of Pop fans was widening: Pop was no longer the province of adolescents. Many of the people who'd rocked to Bill Haley in their wild, free youth had grown up with the music. Pop was still part of their lives. But they'd opted for a peaceful life to which Pop was the background music. In consequence the music they listened to was often dreary (Englebert Humperdink's 'Release me' and 'The last waltz'), or frothy and trivial (The Monkees with their 'A little bit me, a little bit you' and 'Daydream believer'). Sometimes it was coy and sentimental, as with Roger Miller's 'Little green apples'—but always it was warm and comfortable. Rock 'n' Roll might as well never have happened for all the fire and fury that Pop managed to generate at this time.

There were, thankfully, some good Pop records that were well written or cleverly produced. There were songs that had a nodding agreement with passing trends, such as The Move's 'Flowers in the rain' and 'Fire brigade'. There were others, hastily shoved together perhaps, but with a ring of quality or meaning to them—like Cat Stevens's 'I love my dog' and 'Matthew and son'. All these took their place in the blurred overlap area between Pop and Rock.

There always was a large market for run-of-the-mill trivial Pop records. In Britain in 1965, comedian Ken Dodd's whining ballad 'Tears' outsold every single released in that decade except The Beatles' 'She loves you' and 'I want to hold your hand'.

Who were the Pop fans? Pop had become established as mass entertainment. By 1966 it was no longer considered bad taste to listen to Pop. There was a large audience of housewives and mums and dads who tapped their feet with the rest. Generally, the working classes went for Pop because they wanted entertainment that did not make them work too hard. They'd had enough of work by the time they'd clocked off for the day. Since most of the underground or Progressive music was so unorthodox, the conservative middle classes tended to go for Pop, too, with perhaps a little cultured Folk.

In Britain the Mods had given way to the lads who were to become the Skinheads, the bootboys. They roamed the city and small-town streets looking, quite literally, for kicks. These were usually aimed at other gangs or anyone who could be described as a Hippy. They were not so committed to music as their predecessors. They sang their songs, and got their excitement and bruises at soccer matches.

Soul music had become packaged and predictable. The creation of the new Progressive market pushed clubs into changing from Soul to progressive Rock. They lost a large section of their audience in this way and a large number of them folded.

In Hounslow, my home town, there was a club that the Mods had frequented. It opened as the Attic club, changed its name to the Zambesi, then became the Ricky Tick. It went flowery—and the boot-boys did the place over on the first night. It wasn't their scene at all. Already they were getting into Blue-beat, or Ska, West Indian music that eventually came to be known as Reggae.

Many of the Rock musicians and fans were from a different background to the Rock 'n' Roll and Pop fans of the fifties and early sixties. A high proportion of the musicians were college educated, college drop-outs, or people who would have gone on to some form of higher education had the music not claimed them first. Most of the members of Pink Floyd, for example (one of the forerunners of the Rock scene), came from university and art school. Frank Zappa was a graduate. And there were many others. Further education was expanding in Britain and America. Opportunities were being offered to a wider spectrum of people. It was easier, now, for those with little or no money to go to college.

By this stage, the music had reached a sophistication that allowed people to take it seriously. The new breed of college student did not immediately forsake popular culture when he opened his text-books. Rock was telling of *his* experiences and problems. It was talking about politics, and about the coming new world. Universities and colleges were quick to form their own Rock bands and audiences. Because of this new audience, colleges themselves became important as concert venues on the Rock circuit.

Artists saw their music as a personal expression or statement. They took every aspect of it seriously. One significant development was the attitude towards albums. Previously Pop singers usually blasted their way to popularity with a series of hit singles carefully directed to market requirements. Albums were sold on the back of single chart successes. Rock groups, however, saw albums as the real artistic output. Here they could construct series of songs which would give proper vent to their ideas. Concept albums became popular in the wake of early experiments by The Who and, of course, The Beatles' *Sergeant Pepper's Lonely Hearts Club Band*. The concept album gave groups a much greater freedom to explore the music-making innovations and to present a unified piece of music forty or fifty minutes long. In fact singles came to be regarded somewhat disdainfully (at least in public) by many Rock bands.

As this new approach to music developed, a welter of new groups and singers came to the fore in America—Jefferson Airplane, The Grateful Dead, The Doors and Frank Zappa's Mothers of Invention. In Britain, groups like Pink Floyd and Cream appeared. Here, too, Jimi Hendrix first caught public attention. All these artists were album sellers. And they all sold to an audience of young, often college-educated dissidents. All affirmed 'alternative' values. The values and lifestyles taken up by the Rock fraternity are part of what I call the 'New Age Romanticism' of the sixties.

New Age Romanticism
The grand name matches the grandeur of vision that was so much a part of the movement. From 1966 onwards people were prepared to take in 'world-views'. It was a necessity for many of them. A new stage had been reached. Up to this time most of the reactions and ideas about society had been negative ones.

The new age romantics denied the value of the institutions and manifestations of the established culture. They also rejected the culture itself and the foundations on which it was built. That's always the easy thing to do. However, it's impossible to live in a vacuum. Human beings need to know where they stand in relation to the world around them.

There were at the time three groups committed to alternative lifestyles based on alternative world views: the New Left, the Yippies and the Hippy culture. But there were not three separate mutually exclusive movements. Only at the extremes were there sharp differences between them.

The New Left
The New Left was a youth-orientated political movement. It arose out of disenchantment with the liberal, non-violent approach of the Civil Rights Movement because it produced so little result. Members embarked on a process of

'progressive radicalization', ending with an international jamboree of student world riots and sit-ins in 1968.

The New Left was also essentially romantic. In this context, the words of Tom Hayden, the American radical, are revealing. He said: 'We start armed only with questions, believing the answers can be discovered in action.' This was only partly true. The New Left were certain of one main thing: the system they lived under was totally corrupt. It was this certainty which prompted them to act to destroy that order. Like the Civil Rights Movement marchers, they were sure they could change things. They weren't sure how. They had no programme, no unified political alternative to sell. But 'anything's got to be better than this.'

The ideology of the New Left was a patchwork affair. Its following included people from all kinds of political groups: Marxists of all kinds, anarchists, radicalized socialists and pacifists. They were held together only by a common hatred of the forces of law and order and the dream of a new society.

In America the New Left became more and more radical with the escalation of the Vietnam war. Although its dreams of revolution included the working masses, the New Left was a student phenomenon. Its main agents were the SNCC (Student Non-violent Coordinating Committee) and SDS (Students for a Democratic Society). Both had started as pacifist protest organizations, but these origins were no longer recognizable. By 1966 Stokely Carmichael, a militant black nationalist for whom violence was a natural weapon against the forces of reaction, was chairman of SNCC. SDS, too, was not frightened to use violence if necessary.

The New Left came to the conclusion that the only language politicians understood, or used themselves, was the language of power. So it embarked on a policy of confrontation, forcing the government to react. These confrontations, more often than not, took place in the university campuses where even a small group of militants could easily bring a large university to a grinding halt with take-overs and sit-ins.

Being composed of so many elements the New Left carried no unified world view. There was a minimum of coherent thinking about underlying philosophical issues. There was no real interest in the old but important questions about man himself: 'Who is he, where did he come from and where is he going?'

The New Left was out to destroy the existing order, even if it meant chaos. It set to work by means of active subversion, confrontation and if necessary, violence. The extraordinary romanticism of those who belonged to the movement cast a rosy glow on the solutions. Come the revolution, with the economic, social and ethical basis of society completely broken down, a new world would be possible. It was a hugely optimistic dream. It flew in the face of all the evidence of history and of all observable facts about man's own nature.

It was crazy. As if it is ever possible to form a culture with new values out of a disintegrated culture with no transcendent beliefs and no basis for making judgements. The New Left movement failed. It wasn't systematic, it wasn't unified and it was trying to take on industrial nations without the necessary support from the workers. The French students came nearest to victory in Paris in 1968, but they were outmanoeuvred. Even had they managed to destroy a government, what then?

Despite the concern it created in government circles, particularly in America, the New Left was a minority group. It was a small part of the total youth culture. But it had a committed following who made twice as much noise and disruption as anyone else. They knew how to manipulate the media and managed to catch themselves a good share of airtime with their policies of confrontation and outrage. Their influence was a wide one.

They managed to persuade a large mass of young people, if not to join the cause, then at least to maintain a theoretical leftist position. The proliferation of Che Guevara posters on student bedroom walls bore witness to that. Few of those who made such convenient statements of left wing sympathies would have put themselves on the line for revolution. But such was the image and romance of revolution that many young people allowed their fantasies to run that far. It was a symbolic act, the pinning of colours to the mast. By 1972, however, it was quite difficult to get hold of a Che Guevara poster. By that time revolution had ceased to be a saleable commodity.

The New Left movement never really had firm connections with Rock, although inevitably its following bought records. The New Left was a political, polemical organism with specific aims in view. Any music that really reflected its ideas would have to be solidly propagandist. That is what many of the activists wanted. They wanted a music that would put itself behind the cause. As it happened, there were few musicians sufficiently committed or interested to do that. It would inevitably have meant a return to the preachiness of the Protest days, and most people were pretty tired of that.

Of course there was the odd song that caught the spirit of the New Left, for example, The Rolling Stones' 'Street fightin' man': 'The time is ripe for valid revolution.' And there were bands committed to revolution, such as MC5, who brought strange mystical ideas to the old 'power to the people' theme.

Members of the New Left were disappointed in Rock 'n' Roll. They felt it ought, as the art-form of youth culture, to be spearheading their campaign. However, it showed no signs of getting outside the capitalist business system that ran it. Too often, they felt, it concerned itself with themes irrelevant to the overthrow of the system. By their very dissatisfaction with the content, direction and commercial basis of Rock, the New Left showed themselves to be beyond the real sympathies of the mainstream youth culture. Many young people were fairly happy with the prospect of a new society, but they didn't want to be harassed into a revolution. So, apart from the few great occasions of solidarity, such as the 1968 Chicago demonstrations, the New Left failed to mobilize its own peers, let alone the masses. By the early seventies it had ceased to be a real force.

Yippies

The Yippies in America (and the Provos in Holland) were, like the New Left, committed to the destruction of the old order. But they adopted different means to bring it about. Their main weapons were obscenity and humour. They hoped that by submitting straight society to a barrage of insults, obscenities and baffling lampoonery it would collapse in a fit of outrage and humiliation.

Yippies demanded absolute freedom: freedom with a big F. It was the old anarchist dream, a society with no restrictions, no law, no morals. Inevitably the dream never became a reality. So, primarily, the Yippie movement was a destructive one.

Yippies, even more than the New Left, saw the media as a real tool for their use. They weren't especially inclined to use violence, and if it was possible to destroy the structures of society otherwise, then all to the good. They set out to alienate themselves from the mass of the older population by a policy of public outrage.

An important weapon in their armoury was language. In their writings and in public appearances they were deliberately disgusting and obscene. The obscenities were not used without purpose. They were guaranteed to raise the hackles of media controllers and audience alike. They used them symbolically, to shock and anger their audience—but also to abuse the idea of free speech. It was a declaration of freedom—a defiant banner-waving exercise to show that youth more than anyone else knew what it was to be free and say and do whatever they wanted.

But the Yippies also used obscene language deliberately to debase normal language. The movement was not dedicated to the destruction of institutions as the New Left was. It was intent on breaking down the fabric, the values of straight society. Language has always been the basic means of reasoned communication between individuals. It is capable of containing meaning, of carrying great ideas, of describing beauty. It is a lifeline between people. If language is used for ugliness, for degradation and plain evil, it becomes debased. This was one of the distinctive doctrines of the movement. Its purpose was to break down the lines of communication. Reason and logic lost their status becoming, in Yippie terms, outmoded and subjective thinking-processes.

There's no denying that the Yippies were serious about building 'a new everything', even if they were prepared to make humour one of their major weapons. But again the movement gathered only a small following—smaller even than the New Left. Their activities were merry japes, far more entertaining than the pompous rhetoric of the New Left, but no more effective. They wanted sex with anyone they fancied, anytime. They wanted to smoke dope and drop acid. They wanted to canonize Rock 'n' Roll as the official music of the new society, to make pleasure the beginning and the end of life. And they wanted it all on the welfare state.

They saw the world as a gigantic sweet-shop whose contents should be handed over to them. The freedom they demanded was the freedom to gorge themselves stupid—meaningless freedom. It is ironic that a movement dedicated to the debasement of language should destroy the sense of the one word on which they placed any value—freedom.

The Yippies, too, were a little disappointed that Rock did not back them as strongly as they thought it should. The music never quite said what they wanted it to say. A fair example of this happened at the Woodstock Festival, when Pete Townshend of The Who actually kicked Nobie Hoffman, the Yippie luminary, off-stage. Hoffman complained that although The Who had the energy to liberate youth, they weren't adopting the right role in relation to their fans. They weren't revolutionary enough.

Frank Zappa's Mothers of Invention were closer to the Yippie cause—in their use of insults, consciously ugly music, and in cultivating an ugly physical image for themselves. They had albums and films with titles like 'Uncle meat', 'Burnt weenie sandwich', 'Lumpy gravy' and 'Idiot bastard son'. They used the strangest stage props, including dolls, lumps of salami and toy giraffes filled with whipped cream. But this was Zappa's attempt to show how ugly the world actually was, rather than to clear the decks for anarchy. He was much more moderate politically, than his music implied.

Hippies

One of the qualities that characterized the youth movements of the late sixties was a lack of orthodoxy. There was no canon to which anyone could conform. So young dissidents would be quite likely to have sympathies in more than one of the parties searching for alternatives. Some took in all three: New Left, Yippies and Hippies.

Since 1966 the term 'Hippy' has been used almost indiscriminately by journalists: a Hippy may be anyone under thirty with more than half an inch of hair on his head—anyone, in fact, from Jimi Hendrix to Lord Snowdon. But the only people who could really have been called

Frank Zappa
'Closer to the Yippie cause in their use of insults, consciously ugly music and in cultivating an ugly physical image'

Hippies were those who renounced society completely, dropped out, and went to live among others of like mind on a diet of dope, brown rice, music and whatever they could forage.

In 1966–67 the Hippy movement hit the news with an explosion of international love-making, beads and long hair, drugs, flowers and nice smiles coming out to play. Much of the activity was centred on Haight Ashbury in San Francisco. But it didn't last very long. The phenomenon was widely publicized and bamboozled some people into thinking it was the beginning of a new world. But although it was important, it wasn't world-shattering.

At best, Flower Power was a honeymoon, a brief summer of ecstasy on acid. The drug LSD was a key to much of what happened in San Fransisco and elsewhere. Marijuana had been around for quite some time and though it was capable of easing people off, giving them a nice thought or two, it wasn't up to the mind explosions of LSD. Timothy Leary preached acid as the short cut to mind expansion, to a new consciousness, even to God.

Why were so many people ready to accept this? After all, mysticism, love and God weren't exactly fashionable. The music this generation had grown up on was Rock. It was all harsh chords, earthy drums and thudding bass lines—aggressive rebellious stuff. Straight society was a write-off. The young were going to start the new world themselves. But if you've spent all your time denying one set of values, where do you get to pick up a new set when you want them? If this world had been proved inadequate you have to find another. This is what the acid priests were selling. The acid freaks were perhaps the first of the new romantics to opt for an actual alternative, instead of a dream. Acid gave tangible if temporary results.

Leary and his followers were selling mysticism without the discipline, God without the commandments. They preached acid as the path to inner freedom, to a new world inside the head that gave new, magical perception of the world outside. This was just the job for disillusioned youngsters. The fact that many of them had thrown over their parents' religious values didn't mean that they were all unhappy with the idea of religion. Right now they were ready to tackle it again. They desperately needed something to hold on to. They had nothing—no confidence in any institution or leader and no beliefs to speak of. They lived according to norms they despised, in a day-to-day drudgery enlivened only by music and friends. And here was Timothy Leary offering them an experience, not a theology or rules, but an incredible mind-blowing experience that would have its own personal meaning. It was guaranteed to give them a totally new vision of the world. So they took it.

Acid became sacred; it became the answer. It was the way, it lent authority to all statements. When you were tripping you saw the world as it really was, and you saw yourself as a creature capable of great things.

That was the serious side of it. As acid became more widespread, its use became less religious and more frivolous. It became a toy, something to zap the mind out with, a means of fabricating incredible ideas not thought of before. It became the focus of classic 'before and after' stories. 'It wasn't until I took acid that I got it all together' was a common claim.

Much of the Flower Power zeal and basic assumptions were tied in with psychedelics. Before acid, any attempt to suggest seriously that people should all be at peace and should love one another would have been treated with derision (it still was by those outside). The idea that the world would be a better place if everyone got on with one another instead of competing, was not original. Everyone says it from time to time, but it has never seemed possible to persuade everyone to co-operate. Without acid I doubt if anyone would seriously have tried it on. The idea was too naive. Acid, however, provided a convenient optimism along with its visions. While tripping, people could see the answers clearly—so they thought. With their heads open to the universe, they could see that everything was one and that we are all together.

That's why Flower People were so full of terms like 'cosmic consciousness' and 'awareness'. That was the whole thing about acid, it gave a new consciousness—a pseudo-religious awareness of what the world was about. It was because they had this acid experience to lean on that Hippies were able to preach love. They had to have something to base it on, something outside everyday experience —universal love doesn't come naturally to the human race, despite twenty centuries of Christianity.

Acid claimed to be a short cut to perfection. When people realized the dynamic effects it could have on their minds they reacted as if they'd struck gold. The fact that they felt they'd found what they were looking for throws a great deal of light on their search. The freaks of the late sixties weren't looking for a religious experience, despite Paul McCartney's claims to have discovered God. They were trying desperately to find a home in the universe.

It was difficult—impossible—to be properly at home on earth. The 'pigs', the government, even other freaks messed it up. The world was an imperfect place. With acid, however, people thought they'd found home. There was no packing to do, no journeys, it was all inside your head. That was where you went. Even then there was a percentage risk that things could go wrong. A bad trip was tantamount to having your house set on fire.

But this home-inside-your-head was a supreme fallacy. It denied the fact of the real world. Acid-heads, it's true, will say that it simply gave an extra dimension to reality, but that is not quite so. What they got was the final experience that told them what reality was. The acid experience *was* reality. It was the place to be. But it wasn't. It was merely a chemically-induced illusion, a mind scramble. Aldous Huxley once said that the effect of the drug mescaline combined 'all the advantages of Christianity and alcohol (and) none of the defects'. It is a good description. If you imagine a drunken preacher trying to cope with visions of the apocalypse, you get a fair picture of an acid-head describing the world he has just been through.

If it produced any way of coping with the real world it was to attempt an ego-less float through day-to-day life. Even John Lennon, never recognized as a man of small ego, tried to live this way for a while. 'I got a message on acid that you should destroy your ego, and I did . . . I didn't believe I could do anything, and I let people do what they wanted . . . and I just was nothing.'

The love 'n' peace of the Hippies didn't last very long. As the autumn of 1967 drew in, the love craze faded. By that time it had been given world-wide media coverage. The Beatles had brought out a single, 'All you need is love'. A mysterious dressed-up Hippy called Scott McKenzie recorded a fatuous song, 'Let's go to San Francisco', which sold a lot in Britain. The Stones brought out a concept album, *Their Satanic majesties request*, which proved to be the wettest piece of music they'd ever recorded. For a short while they were thoroughly overtaken by the plague of whimsy which blew in a wave over the music scene.

Acid had quite an effect on the music. Whereas Protest and then Dylan's later records made song-writers think about how they wrote, acid had a fair amount to do with the actual content of the songs. I'm not saying that all, or even most, of the Rock songs written at this time were written on or were directly related to drugs of any kind. But it did have an effect of widening the perspective of song-writers. There was a crop of dreamlike songs, for instance, The Beatles'

'Lucy in the Sky with Diamonds' (not necessarily a drug song but the influence is there). Also Procul Harum's 'Whiter shade of pale' with lines like this:

> 'We skipped the light fandango
> And turned cartwheels cross the floor
> I was feeling kind of seasick
> But the crowd called out for more.'

Donovan, a British Folk/Protest singer, went all warm and misty, and Eric Burdon, late of The Animals, turned from a sweaty, Blues growler to a post-acid peace-loving Hippy with an awful record, 'San Franciscan nights'.

Then there were the more violent groups, some of whom attempted a light/sound simulation of an acid trip. Such groups were The Grateful Dead and Jefferson Airplane. There were other bands who perhaps weren't so positively drug-oriented, such as The Doors, Quicksilver Messenger Service, Cream and Pink Floyd. But for most of them dope, pills and acid were there in the background. Most of them smoked and almost as many took acid; but not all of them went further than that, though all kinds of drugs were easily available in Rock circles and fairly widely used.

What relation had Rock music to the rise of drug-use among young people? Paranoid statements have been made by people trying to analyse Rock lyrics in order to point out obscure references to marijuana and the like. At the same time innocent disclaimers were made by some of the Rock fraternity. But it's plainly obvious that Rock musicians were using drugs of all kinds some time before it caught on among young people. Everyone knew they smoked and, as the weed became widely distributed, so did their fans. However, it is a fact, not always recognized, that many of the major groups and musicians, particularly in the States, have made public statements or even appeared in advertisements spelling out the dangers of hard drugs such as heroin and amphetamines.

When the Hippy honeymoon was over, it didn't mean an end to the new consciousness. It was the beginning. Peace 'n' love and Flower Power were really the first flush of enthusiasm. In Haight Ashbury, love had lasted only as long as there was enough to go round. With so many kids wandering around trying to live on hand-outs, crashing out wherever there was a space, the resources soon dwindled. Slowly the place turned into a squalid slum and the 'beautiful people' drifted away.

In Britain, the whole thing had been a bit of a Carnaby Street type novelty, existing more in the imaginations of the press than anywhere else. There were, however, ripples in the music business and literally hundreds of magazines sprang up on both sides of the Atlantic. Some lasted only an issue or two and some, like *Rolling Stone*, are still going. There were alternative bookshops, alternative restaurants, everything—all heading in the same direction.

An eclectic culture

The music, too, had a common direction, but it never had a common strategy or basis. One of the factors that most characterized the underground was its eclecticism. There was room for hundreds of shades of opinion and belief within the sub-culture.

Rock contained most if not all of them. It had a dynamic relationship with the largest part of the underground population. The Rock audience was not predominantly political, neither was it committed in any firm sense to the drop-out tactics of Hippies. It comprised the large mass of young people who, in theory at least, were prepared to defy the authority of their elders and were in sympathy with the idea that they themselves could create a new society based on different values.

The music they listened to was just the same. The

Eric Clapton
'Sweeping the crowd along, up, and into the music with his lightening and sometimes painful guitar solos'

musicians they worshipped were individually part of the same complex of ideals and lifestyles.

For instance, George Harrison brought his particular eastern flavour to the music—with his 'Within you without you' on the Beatles' 'Sergeant Pepper' album. Captain Beefheart appeared, with his curious rasping voice, offering a peculiar surrealist view of the world. Then Cream blasted off at a shattering level of decibels with Eric Clapton sweeping the crowd along, up, and into the music with his lightning and sometimes painful guitar solos. The actual content of the songs was less than important. They were only a vehicle for the Blues-based musical energies of Eric Clapton, Ginger Baker and Jack Bruce. But the sound provided a sort of subliminal violence with which their audience could physically involve themselves.

The Beach Boys, or at least Brian Wilson their songwriter, had found a musical streak and created the undeniably beautiful 'Good vibrations'. It was a love song, but Wilson threw in the good vibrations phrase, very much a slogan of the period—everyone getting vibes of one kind or another off everything.

The Stones brought a flavour of the occult to the Rock scene with their album *Their Satanic majesties request* though it was probably more pun than voodoo. And their Song 'Sympathy for the devil' had an obvious occult focus. The Stones showed that the sinister was as much part of the trip as the serene.

The Band turned up in the late sixties with their first album, *Music from big pink*. This at first proved more influential among musicians than among the audience. They rocked, but with a decidedly Country flavour. This countrified easing-off was a symptom of the growing desire to leave the cities behind.

Then, of course, Blood, Sweat and Tears brought a strong, if clichéd Jazz influence to Rock. Paul Simon brought a poetry of human relationships. Leonard Cohen brought a depressing, indulgent existentialism to the scene. And Sly and the Family Stone put some Soul into it, as did Joe Cocker.

Why was the Rock culture so eclectic? Again it comes back to rootlessness. The Rock people had no traditions of their own, only a short-lived musical history and a background of struggle against the beliefs of the previous generation. The only 'ideology' they had was the basic assumption that it was better to get along with one another than to compete. But out of this desire to create a free co-operative society, came a search through world religions and cultures to find any clues as to how to make it a reality. A search in one direction by The Beatles, Donovan and others led to Transcendental Meditation. Others went for different flavours of Eastern mysticism. They felt that Eastern philosophy had a serenity, a oneness with the universe and a spiritual quality that was lacking in the West's technological culture.

Acid experiences tended towards the mystical, and it was no coincidence that Timothy Leary put together a book or two of psychedelic prayers. People started drifting off to all points East—to India, Turkey and Afghanistan—half in search of spiritual enlightenment and half in search of a country without dope-laws. From 1966 onwards there was a trickle working up to a torrent of young doper/mystics on the Eastern trail.

Another alternative, that seemed attractive to the New Romantics, was the call of the wild. There was a surge in the direction of the country. There was a feeling that if people could get back to mother earth, to a simpler homespun existence, then the problems and tensions created by cities would be over. For some it was a semi-mystical desire, prompted by a belief that the earth was basically good and modern technology had corrupted it: 'We are stardust, we are golden . . . and we've got to get back to the garden', as

Joni Mitchell put it.

But for some the return to the country was simpler. Bob Dylan had a brief country brush with albums like *Nashville skyline* and *New morning*. For him and others, like The Byrds, country life was simply a matter of waking up to trees rather than traffic. It was the pastoral effect of the country they sang about, not one man and his involvement with the soil. Dylan even took on board the rounded sentimental clichés of the Country and Western singer on *Nashville skyline*: 'Love is all there is, it makes the world go round.' This was honey love, not the universal version that the Hippies preached.

Not everyone was prepared to take on the whole of the Eastern trip. And not many were happy or able to move out of the cities. Some became Zen Buddists in New York or joined the Radha Krishna temple in London; others were less particular.

Tolerance

The drift around the world, the readiness to borrow from all kinds of cultures blended into a new, still dominantly western, underground culture with music at its centre. Everyone was into the music at an almost religious level. For the first time in its short history the music became much more important to a large proportion of young people than TV. American kids went to Rock concerts instead of drive-ins. There were radio stations who played nothing but Rock. In Britain, pirate off-shore radio stations played continuous Pop, twenty-four hours a day. Most of it was top-forty but the very quantity of music coming across the air-waves meant that more Progressive and unusual records were able to take their chance.

Despite the mix of foreign bloods flowing into the music, and despite the hotchpotch of ideas surrounding it, it was still Rock. It has always been essentially gut-level, hard-driven music—basically aggressive, or at least active.

Place that against the tolerance of the dope-culture and it doesn't seem to add up. There were, of course, bands and individuals who played gentle music. The Lovin' Spoonful, for instance, with songs like 'Do you believe in magic?' and 'What a day for a daydream'. George Harrison managed to promote interest in the sitar player Ravi Shankar and groups like The Incredible String Band brought a spirit of mystical whimsy and a smell of incense to the Folkie end of the Rock scene. However few people were able to take the twangings of Ravi Shankar or the elfin tones of the String Band as the whole of their musical diet. Most had to play a little of that then perhaps a bit of the Stones, who by 1968 had left Flower Power behind and released a piece of tough, explosive arrogance in the form of 'Jumping jack flash'. It was all very well being mellow or tranquil for a while, but a regular adrenalin charge was necessary.

The Beatles had a brief developing stage including a kind of Carnaby Street jollity with 'When I'm sixty-four', 'Penny Lane' and 'Your Mother should know'. They had their more reflective moments, shown in 'Eleanor Rigby' 'Strawberry Fields' and 'Fool on the hill'. They played kiss-chase with the Hippies with 'All you need is love', and then got tired of it. Like The Stones, they felt the need for some oomph in their, by now, top-heavy productions and produced a simple Rocker, 'Lady Madonna'. Did this return to a punchy style indicate disillusionment with all attempts at peaceful co-existence? I don't think so. The new consciousness emphasized self-awareness. This kind of self-searching found those reserves of adrenalin or aggressive instincts which musicians naturally gave vent to. For instance The Who's 'I can see for miles' is an acid song but it's not all calm contemplation. Keith Moon's speed-freak drumming denies that; its practically manic. So while there was an interlude of meditation in music, it faded like Flower Power.

Too much whimsy and contemplation produces flabby

Jimi Hendrix
'He wasn't a lone performer, fooling about up on stage—there was an explosion of energy felt as much by the audience as Hendrix'

music. Rock began in reaction to a similar situation with the music of the thirties, thriving on muscle and excitement. What the music of the late sixties did was largely to channel that aggression in a creative rather than a destructive way. So Jimi Hendrix would attack a song, wrestling with his guitar so that it was all but bent out of shape. Who was he wreaking his vengeance on? Not his audience, not the guitar. When Hendrix set fire to his guitar at Monterey in 1967 it was an exposition. It was the demonstration of power, energy and potential. This was where the audience and the performer came into a positive relationship. He wasn't a lone performer, fooling about up on stage—there was an explosion of energy felt as much by the audience as by Hendrix. They had power as a united body of consciousness brought together by their youth. With music as fiery and terrible as this the world was already conquered.

Although the violence of the music served to unify the ranks of youth, rather than to attack the establishment, it wasn't about to throw any bouquets to the straights. Any love and co-operation there might have been was shared among the sub-culture. It wasn't about to extend the franchise outside the circle. This is an essential characteristic of the underground culture. It was a celebration of itself. The violence and decibel level of its music worked for those already into Rock. Although it wasn't consciously intended, the crushing decibel level of bands like Cream and The Who was guaranteed to alienate the older generation. Much of the noise and aggression of this kind of Rock was sheer exuberance. But it was also a kind of sublimation of the violence and frustration felt by the musicians.

There wasn't that much aggro in the air. Audiences went to have a good time, to be lifted by the music, and carried along by its flow, like riding over rapids. The real trip was simply to let go of everything else and be carried away by the music. In the States a good proportion of the audiences of bands like The Grateful Dead, The Doors and Iron Butterfly were stoned before they came. It was all part of loosing their hold on gritty unpleasant reality and being floated off somewhere.

Until about 1966 Pop fans danced *dances*. There were recognized names and recognized steps. Naturally, as the development of Pop speeded up, new dances and steps arrived, some of them predictably short-lived. Remember the twist, the frug, the jerk, the locomotion and the hitchhiker? They moved progressively further away from courtship rituals towards the expressions of individual style favoured by the Mods.

For Rock fans of the late sixties dancing was different again. Like the Mods, dancers tended to move individually rather than in couples. It was not a display. Dancing came from an identification with the music. Individuals found themselves a space to gyrate or shake their heads or simply leap about. 'Idiot dancers' we called, them, because they looked unhinged; completely crazed on the sound. There were no steps and there was no form. It was just one person's body plugged into the music.

Forward!

The energy of the music was to a large extent rooted in R & B. There had been a big Blues boom in both Britain and the States from 1966–67, bringing to the surface white Blues groups such as John Mayall's Blues Breakers, Canned Heat, Paul Butterfield's Blues Band and Fleetwood Mac. But by now the music was more integrated into a distinct culture. Already the underground was being called the Rock culture, giving recognition to the central importance of the music for a large proportion of young people.

There was a great deal of excitement flying about. Everyone was sure they were on the verge of something big. Rock music took and extended this excitement, giving it tangibility. Words became less important as the music developed. Just a few slogans here and there were enough. Blistering hot guitar solos did the rest. Rock made a supportive musical environment for the culture. Concerts were the clan gatherings, and festivals were great celebrations, of the new lifestyle. There was a band or a singer for every mood, as well as for every quirk or weirdism. But they were all going in the same direction: forward.

The late sixties, as we have already seen, was a time of searching. The search began as a spiritual one. Young people set out to find answers to the big questions and to found a new society built on real values, where people could be free from oppression and convention, free from the necessity to work.

For a while they found it. But the seekers who went to the East came back thinner, with only a worn veneer of mysticism. Acid-heads, having found 'home' inside themselves, discovered that it was confusing and unreliable. Communes broke up over personal conflicts and the dope-heads found that being chased by the law wasn't fun. Generally they settled into a 'semi-alternative' existence, a happy medium—a happy summer holiday in the city. It was a bit inadequate, but they wouldn't make it to the freedom of the country *this* year. Instead of really going for comprehensive answers to the big questions—Who am I? Where do I come from? Where am I going?—they settled for less, as people so often do. And many of them opted for fulfilment.

Truth is something a bit too big to tackle. It requires commitment. The New Age Romantics wanted freedom *and* fulfilment. Eastern religions were stylish and, in their westernized forms cheap on discipline. Many wanted this kind of pocket-sized spirituality. It didn't get in the way.

Above all people wanted the easy life. Life was to be enjoyed and if a blended mysticism helped, that was all right. If dope helped, that was OK. Music helped and that was fine. But no one wanted a heavy truth trip. That was too claustrophobic.

The years 1966–69 saw a generation trying, like the children of Israel, to assemble its flocks and herds to leave Egypt. It was difficult because, though there were heroes and orators, there were no leaders and there was no authority or doctrine. It was a shambling rabble with an intense energy and an idealism, but only a generalized sense of direction. They were held together by the knowledge that they thought and felt differently from their parents; they were going somewhere else.

The Animals hit of 1965—a different period—is strangely apt:

> 'We've gotta get out of this place
> If it's the last thing we ever do
> We've gotta get out of this place
> Gonna find a better life for me and you'.

The city is not a good place to spend the summer. Next year they might spend some time in the country. Little did they know that they were headed for a wilderness as barren as the city streets.

5
Summer can't be beat
(1969-72)

At the beginning of this time some extravagant claims were made about the significance of the underground culture. By the end of it these claims were seen to be illusory. Those who sensed the way the wind was blowing saw the Rock culture fading in 1971.

What I thought at the time was a movement towards an alternative lifestyle—which though I couldn't wholeheartedly endorse, I sympathized with—turned out to be an elaborate protest. I involve myself here because then, more than at any previous time, I felt myself part of the new generation. The naive excesses of Flower Power had seemed both glib and unworkable. The New Left had been too serious and too militant, the Yippies too destructive and obscene, for my tender sensibilities.

By 1969 the scene had calmed to the point where I could fit in on the fringes of things. Rock culture had an atmosphere of tolerance. There was room for everyone, even for Christians it seemed. And although I now see it rather differently, it was an exciting and important time for me.

I believed a lot of the PR. Some mates of mine were

starting a band around that time, struggling for recognition. This gave me a special feeling of involvement. I felt that Rock was the spearhead of a new culture. I was sure it was better than the establishment I'd grown to despise.

Theodore Roszak's book *The Making of a Counter Culture* came out in 1969. Perhaps the most significant thing he said was this: 'If the resistance of the counter culture fails I think there will be nothing in store for us but what anti-utopians like Huxley and Orwell have forecast'. I half-believed that, and even though I didn't discover the quote until a year or two later, it was an idea that had been nagging at the back of my mind.

The important word, it seems to me now, was 'resistance'. That is really what the Rock culture was about. The 'revolution' never happened. The Rock culture flattered itself, contending that it was culture in its own right, set up in opposition to the establishment. In the period between 1969 and 1971 it got as near as it ever would to that claim. I don't think it ever really made it.

The Music

It is important to understand that Rock was widely regarded as art. Not everyone talked about it in high art terms, but it was taken seriously. Bob Dylan, with his move from Protest to poetry, and The Beatles with their *Sergeant Pepper* album had made that breakthrough.

A large part of Rock's appeal was its ability to reflect the experience of living at that time in the twentieth century, to say something relevant to its generation. Modern 'classical' music was a non-starter in this respect. *Avant-garde*, despite its name, made no real dent in the alternative culture.

Jazz was chuntering along in its own sub-culture. Small revivalist and modern Jazz units did their stints in pub bars and in the dwindling number of Jazz clubs. In the concert halls, the big stars trotted out their arpeggios, sometimes with artistry and sometimes even with inspiration, but not with any real relevance.

There were, of course, Jazz buffs among Rock musicians. In Britain, The Soft Machine got fairly serious and pretty boring with its preoccupation with relatively free-form Jazz. In the States there were always Chicago and Blood Sweat and Tears, both of whom saw it as more of a romp than anything else—a chance to get a full brassy sound.

Rock rules OK

Rock was the music of the moment. Jazz and the *avant-garde* were making music about music. Rock was making music about living. That didn't mean every song was about 'life', with meaningful lyrics about man's struggle to come to terms with his predicament. The lyrics weren't always important. It was the feeling that they had common enemies and common frustrations that brought performer and audience together—plus a shared enthusiasm for exciting music. Communication was a matter of intuition rather than direct language.

Symbols and symbolic acts were an important part of the communication. By burning an American flag a Rock band could trigger a roar of approval and shouts of 'right on' from the audience. It was a gesture, everyone knew what it meant and how to respond. That was the kind of solidarity that became a part of the Rock culture. It was a shared experience—*us* against *them*.

It was the use of symbols, of catch phrases, and an implicit enmity towards the establishment that made Rock such a significant force in forging the counter-culture. Jan Wenner, editor of *Rolling Stone,* a paper that did more than any other to build Rock into the focus of the underground, said that *Rolling Stone* was founded in the belief that Rock was 'the energy centre' for change: social, political and cultural. I agreed, although I didn't much want to because I thought that that was what Christianity ought to be doing, but wasn't. Rock culture, I felt, was teaching Christianity a lesson.

Image and charisma

In Rock invention and improvization were essential. 'Feel' was as much a deciding-point as to whether a song worked or not as any other. But in another sense this denial of rational thinking was an effective 'get-out' for the Rock culture. It meant you didn't have to work anything out. You just did it.

This was where symbolic acts and catch phrases came in useful. A performer could do something on stage—drop his trousers, or say 'All politicians are liars', or, as in the oft-quoted song of The Doors, sing 'We want the world and we want it now'. The press might quiz him about it, but it would be taken largely at face value. The audience didn't ask for explanations, they just went 'yeah'. So there was a kind of intuitive response between performer and audience. People then started to talk about the music being a universal language. I think that was exaggerated, but it's possible to see why folk said it. The thing that puzzled everyone was that Rock was very difficult to talk about. It was possible to talk about a singer's range or what he sang about, but Rock was always more than the sum of its parts. That was why John Sebastian, in his song 'Do you believe in magic?', said: 'It's like trying to tell a stranger about Rock 'n' Roll.' It's not possible; it has to be experienced.

From the very beginning of Rock 'n' Roll, image was a fundamental ingredient of performance. It would be difficult to overestimate its importance. In the fifties, singers were expected to be mean, moody and magnificent. In the age of Rock, although they were still expected to have charisma, they had to be able to make some kind of social comment. They didn't have to be activists, nor did they have to be consistent, but they had to say the right things. And they were often only too keen to talk.

The fact that Rock stars were known to have views on Vietnam, ideas about personal freedom, or beliefs in astrology, obviously influenced their music. John Lennon was once asked if he planned to write any anti-war songs and he said 'all our songs are anti-war songs'. It was a dumb question. Everyone knew what The Beatles and John Lennon, in particular, stood for. It was in their music, in 'universal language'. But part of the reason why Rock and its culture never got to the revolution was that it wasn't so much a language as a shorthand.

The Rock press, particularly *Rolling Stone*, did a crucial back-up job on the music's image. The papers provided detailed biographies and background material on artists. They featured exclusive interviews in which stars gave their opinions on every subject under the sun. Little went on in the Rock world that was not reported. This service, far from dispelling the superstar myths of the Rock fraternity, contrived to heighten the mystique.

All this background information conspired to make the prominent Rock figures into oracles. *Rolling Stone*, for instance, regularly featured a major interview. These had a tremendous influence on the audiences. They shaped their idea about what the stars were like, and they shaped the readers' own opinions. Even little snippets were important. A friend once told me he'd first read Truman Capoté's *In Cold Blood* because he'd seen a photo of Brian Jones of The Rolling Stones with a copy. I can remember studying the cover to Dylan's *Blonde on blonde* album in order to tie my scarf right. It was all a part of a desire to borrow some of their style, some of their charisma.

There is no denying that many of the major performers of the Rock culture period had real charisma. Jimi Hendrix, John Lennon, Eric Clapton and many more, were figures of considerable presence. On stage they commanded attention on a purely musical level and were capable of leading an audience wherever they wanted.

Combine that potential, and the inevitable curiosity of their fans, with a Rock press that was prepared to treat their political, moral and social ideas with the same serious attention as they did their music, and you have oracles in the making. Rock stars were therefore more than entertainers. They were heroes. Fans put them on a pedestal because of their musical magic.

The combination of the performer's personal expression and the audience's identification with him was explosive. If, say, Country Joe McDonald of Country Joe and the Fish were to say, 'This song's dedicated to the fascists who run our country', the audience wouldn't analyse his statement for accuracy or weigh up what he said. People would say 'yeah, kill the pigs', or something like that. It was mindless, but this wasn't a seminar. And both the audience and the performers knew what they thought about politics before they entered the hall. It was simply a matter of celebrating the cause—declaring solidarity.

Rock festivals recreated the same feelings but on a larger scale and over a longer period. The Woodstock festival was so successful that 'Woodstock Nation' was a serious appellation. Unfortunately not all festivals were quite so surrounded by love and affection as Woodstock. At Altamont, in ugly scenes with the Hells Angels, one person was stabbed to death. But that was an extreme.

The good vibes and the rapport that was achieved between musicians and audiences, both at concerts and festivals, began to persuade some people that Rock 'n' Roll was a kind of cure-all. 'Rock 'n' Roll is the answer' became an almost familiar cry. I don't know who got the idea first, whether it was the audience or the musicians—but the feeling grew that since Rock was drawing all the crowds together and keeping them happy, Rock ought to be at the base of the new culture. As this generation moved on, as it gathered in strength with Rock as its rallying-point, and youth took over (and presumably got older) the Rock generation would be in the driving-seat. Rock would be the official music of the populace.

Musicians felt that the music had expanded so far that it was capable of soaking up whatever new musical direction came along. Everyone was so knocked out with Rock, they thought it just had to go on for ever.

Names

At the risk of repeating names already mentioned in previous chapters, it's worth putting the spotlight on a few Rock figures who were most active, or talkative, during the period from 1969 to 1971.

The Who and Pete Townshend were at the centre of the Rock culture. Townshend was a consistent interviewee who really believed in Rock 'n' Roll. At certain times he has shown himself to be an accurate prophet. In 1968 he said: 'Rock 'n' Roll is going to become down home, it's gonna become realistic. It's going to become the answer to the day's problems. It's going to become part of everybody's life from now on.'

That was what happened. People used their record collections that way. During these highpoint years The Who toured constantly, on both sides of the Atlantic. They were one of the most dynamic acts ever, to see live. Townshend, as a spokesman and a musician, was tremendously respected by other musicians. And he was hero-worshipped by the fans. In a TV interview as late as mid 1972, Steve Howe of Yes was asked what future developments he saw in music. His reply, only half-joking, was 'It depends on what Townshend does next'.

Townshend claimed to have found some kind of repose in

the teachings of Meher Baba. It was very influential in the more religious aspects of The Who's Rock opera *Tommy*. He wrote a fascinating song, released in 1970 as a single called 'The seeker', detailing a semi-personal search for truth.

> 'I'm looking for me.
> You're looking for you.
> We're looking at each other
> and we don't know what to do.'

The Rolling Stones were still going strong. They'd recovered from their limp-wrist period around 1967, and were back making tough Rock 'n' Roll. Brian Jones died in 1969, one of the first of a number of Rock deaths (both Jimi Hendrix and Janis Joplin were to follow). In 1970 The Stones released *Let it bleed*, still my favourite Stones album. In the 1969–70 period they were touring constantly and, like The Who, these high-excitement performances placed them at the top of the Rock culture hierarchy.

Jimi Hendrix was in decline in 1969–70. His last fully-fledged album was *Electric ladyland*. His big years were 1967–68, but his figure and influence stayed on in the Rock culture years. Ironically, his death in 1970 gave him a new boost of much-needed publicity. He was probably the last single hero figure of the Rock culture. He was the ultimate guitar-hero, having all the presence, the sensuality, the voice and the song-writing ability, as well as his unbelievable guitar-playing. He was really into power music, with lyrics like:

> 'I was standing next to a mountain
> chop it down with the edge of my hand.'

Crosby, Stills, Nash and Young were the quintessential Rock culture group. They were adept within soft harmony accoustic Folk and raunchy Country style Rock 'n' Roll.

Crosby, Stills, Nash and Young
'Were stuffed full of idealism.... They stood for everything their audience wanted them to'

They were stuffed full of idealism. They more than anyone, got through to what young people were feeling. They were prepared to deal with issues as they came up. They wrote the song 'Ohio' straight after the shootings at Kent State University. Neither were they ashamed of crass banality as in 'Almost cut my hair' on the *Deja Vu* album—a song of teenage paranoia if ever I heard one. If Hendrix was the last guitar hero, CSN&Y were the last real Folk heroes of the Rock culture. They had all the right clichés and the right beliefs, and they stood for everything their audience wanted them to. When asked what they thought the youth culture had achieved they said, 'We stopped a war, man!'

The record business

Were the record companies responsible for discovering, packaging and selling Rock to an unsuspecting public? Or did the audience demand for Rock 'n' Roll stimulate the record industry into supplying the demand and so increase profits?

Things have changed since the early Rock 'n' Roll records. In those days an artist had very little, if any, creative control, over his material. But that's only half the story. The record companies may have been able to control their artists, but they could never be sure that what they gave their artists to sing would please the public.

The public, fortunately, had enough individuality and quirks of taste not to be steam-rollered by the record companies' output. Obviously record buyers could choose only from what was released to them. But if they didn't like any of them, they weren't obliged to buy. It was a fragile balance between audience demand and company anticipation of taste. It is interesting to note that most of the musical booms this side of World War II, the R & B boom, the Rock 'n' Roll boom, and the Folk boom, all started off as minority interests. The interest began to grow, and the record companies cashed in.

Inevitably there was exploitation and manipulation. But the Rock/Pops audience had a remarkable knack of spotting the genuine article. As Rock 'n' Roll developed into Pop and on into Progressive Rock, artists were given more creative freedom. Companies began to realize that, often, the people who really had their fingers on the pulse of the market were the artists themselves. The Beatles made one of the early breakthroughs. Although he contributed a great deal to their music, Beatles' producer George Martin was sensible enough to see that their own songs and musical ideas were better than any he could manufacture for them.

As artists like The Beatles became world famous, and therefore vitally important to the record companies, and as performers began to take a much more serious view of their own musical development and their own artistic statements, the companies were willing to give them a freer hand. They hoped to keep artists happy and that way ensure that contracts were renewed. But there were still squabbles and many unhappy marriages.

Things became very sensitive, especially during and after the Protest boom. Artists were using company money and publicity to promote a cause directly opposed to the aims of the record industry. Groups like Jefferson Airplane were singing 'tear down the wall' and MC5 were saying even nastier things. It seemed that Rock was aiming to destroy the fabric from which the record industry was made.

During the most embarrassing years, the big record companies seemed to pursue a policy of enlightened self-interest. They valued the revenue of even their most revolutionary artists. In some cases both artists and companies felt they were being used, but generally the artists were left alone.

But the record companies did manipulate their artists in

the top forty singles market. They manufactured groups, found singers and provided them with material. They picked performers who had no axe to grind and were content to churn out the material—as long as the money kept flowing in.

With new groups, on a first contract, record companies attempted to get as much control of their artists as possible; but they trod warily. So during the years 1967–71 the performers really had the best of the deal. They were making music for a large audience and record sales often meant that they could demand whatever they wanted from the record companies. In the late sixties, several firms took on what came to be known as 'company freaks' or 'house Hippies'—ex-underground journalists and ex-Rock group managers. It was their job to effect liaison between the company and the underground press and also to act as talent scouts. It worked reasonably well because the artists needed the companies and companies needed the artists.

The only area in which record companies tended to censor was that of display materials. For instance, Decca asked The Rolling Stones to change the cover design for the *Beggars banquet* album in 1968. It was considered bad taste. The Stones reluctantly complied. But Decca would never have dared ask them to change any of their music. Several of John Lennon's words were asterisked on the lyric sheet of his *John Lennon and the Plastic Ono band* album, because the album sleeves would be on public display. It was a fairly insignificant area of control.

The late sixties saw a rash of Rock stars beginning their own labels, so ensuring total artistic freedom. Rolling Stones Records is one example, The Beatles' Apple another. They simply used the bigger companies for distribution purposes.

As times became leaner, record companies began to play safe. They were less willing to give out new contracts, or to renew old ones for more established artists who were failing to sell.

Success

The inspiring thing about the Rock culture was always the element of challenge. I imagine guerrillas must feel the same kind of excitement in taking on an enemy more organized and better equipped than themselves. The Rock culture —like the guerrillas—took its stand on what it was against, rather than what it was for. Battles for independence were fought and won. By the late sixties rigid standards of dress and appearance had been broken. There was also a much more casual attitude to sexual behaviour. Perhaps the biggest political victory of the counter culture was the decision of the United States finally to withdraw from Vietnam. Another big drive of the underground was the legalization of marijuana. They did not succeed in this. But sentences became lighter and pressure built up on the police to concentrate on the hard stuff, heroin and cocaine.

The Rock culture questioned everything straight society offered. Politicians were less respected as a breed at the beginning of the seventies than they had been ten years earlier. In 1974 came the Watergate scandal. Of all the media, only the underground press had consistently attacked President Nixon as a liar and a power maniac. This was a moral victory for them. Authority had been discredited.

The culture left a definite mark. It succeeded both as a social shake-up and as a cultural revolution. The generation had relentlessly challenged whatever they came up against. It was a bold attempt at breathing new life into a compromised, hypocritical society that seemed to have lost its sense of life. The Rock culture challenged the church too and, though it hurt me as a Christian, I knew that the substance of its challenge was right. The church had to a large extent lost its commitment as a truly radical and revolutionary body. Many Christians had mindlessly accepted a materialist status quo. Culturally the church was well nigh dead; it was in danger of losing its voice in the twentieth century.

But Rock culture was only a pre-revolutionary, resistance culture. Once the goals were reached, there was nothing left. Rock culture died because it was brought up on fighting battles. Ever since the fifties, Rock had been a resistance movement against the older generation. As history progressed the battles became more significant, and the Rock culture became stronger and more wily in its strategy. Then, without anyone fully understanding it, the Rock culture had won its major battles and there wasn't anything left to fight about. With nothing to fight for there was nothing to say, nothing to make music about. And so the Rock culture began to disintegrate.

6

(1972-)

The Rock culture won all the battles but lost the war. That's what it looked like in the early seventies. The music was still good but something was missing. The strength of the Rock culture had been built on the fact that everyone was going in the same direction. A mass of people were generally agreed on what was wrong and what major changes were necessary. But they were not sure what to do after that.

The 'alternative society' was not in fact an alternative society, it was more a network of alternative individuals. The alternative society was a myth, a dream. When the forces of youth claimed they were ready to take over, they didn't know the half. The Rock culture misled itself into thinking it had the answers when really it had only the questions.

The key to the failure lies, I believe, in the Dream City of Woodstock, New York State, 1969. For one weekend Woodstock became the third largest 'city' in the state, but it was a disaster area in more senses than one. I feel it gives certain valuable clues about the make-up of the Rock culture. It was eulogized as an expression of the new nation in Joni Mitchell's song 'Woodstock';

By the time we got to Woodstock we were half a million strong
And everywhere was a song and a celebration;
And I dreamed I saw the bomber-death-planes riding shotgun in the sky;
Turning into butterfles above our nation.'

People had trekked miles to Yasgur's Farm leaving the deathly cities, and the cramping society that made them, far behind. They had a ball. Three days of dope, sex and music. Despite the rain and the mud—and no food—they felt they'd hit paradise. This was what it was going to be like when the dream came true. . .

I was greatly saddened by the film of Woodstock. It showed a prevailing herd mentality. Eat, copulate and sleep—a completely consumer-based hedonistic diet. Obviously it was a festival, and people weren't there to do much else. But they seemed extraordinarily self-satisfied. There was a kind of helplessness, combined with a built-in expectation that somehow someone was going to bail them out. Fortunately community groups like the Hog Farm did just that. Also extra supplies were flown in and handed out. Otherwise peace might not have prevailed.

I should have known then that these were no makers of a new society. The kids who were wandering about gleefully saying, 'Hey man, we're a disaster area', weren't about to build anything.

A society, a culture has to be built from principles. But it must also have concrete ideas. The Rock culture had principles of a vague, humanitarian kind. It also had ideas, but only a handful of individuals had the personal commitment to turn them into realities. The majority wanted an end to the war, an end to this and that—then into free space.

The leaders weren't really leaders at all. They were catalysts or hero-figures. Jagger, Townshend, Crosby, Stills,

Nash and Young were all musicians with charisma. They were idealists. But they couldn't take the generation anywhere. They were too much a part of it. They were spokesmen. They stood for what the people believed. To a degree they were sincere. But they couldn't lead anyone out of a paper bag. And they were quite ready to admit it.

Rock culture in the seventies, like the audience at Woodstock, went back home. Faced with the necessity to readjust, it disintegrated.

John Lennon, by now on his own, and as transparent as ever, summed it up. Heavy with sadness and resignation he sang:

'The dream is over, what can I say,
the dream is over, yesterday.'

There is no convenient point at which the belief and the optimism disappeared, or after which the Rock culture died. Don McLean in his epic song 'American Pie' attempts to say that the Altamont Festival was 'the day the music died'; but that's too convenient. It simply showed up the darker side of human nature and sowed some doubts in people's minds.

Dylan and Lennon—farewell

Rock stars had almost always been ahead of the audience. They brought new ideas to their followers and the fans trailed behind them. It happened with clothes, with dope, with long hair, and then with fragmentation.

Dylan was probably the first to go. Until 1968, despite a long lay-off because of a near-fatal motorcycle accident, he still retained his position as one of the most influential of Rock figures. The statistics tell us that he didn't, in fact, sell a lot of records. Nevertheless, fellow musicians as well as the music press had their attitudes and musical values developed through his songs.

Most of Dylan's music up to and including *John Wesley*

Harding in 1968 was a sane commentary on life itself. This album contained the characteristic dark images and strange personalities that were Dylan's unique feature.

There was only a mere inkling on the album of what was to come. It was embodied in the last cut on the album, a song called 'I'll be your baby tonight'. It was Country, unashamedly simple and sentimental:

> 'That big fat moon is gonna shine like a spoon
> But we're gonna let it
> You won't regret it.'

In 1969 Dylan released his tenth album, *Nashville skyline*. Dylan's albums always drew much attention. This one caused unparalleled controversy. What was he doing? For a second time Dylan's fans felt betrayed.

This time he seemed to have gone mindless. The album had been recorded in Nashville, the American capital of Country music with resident Country musicians. *Nashville skyline* was light-hearted, melodic and quite without the nightmare visions fans were used to. *Nashville skyline*, enjoyable as it is, was a deliberate attempt to see the world as just a simple place where people fall in love, break up, play music and eat country pie. It was a bid to ignore the mystery and overwhelming complexity of the world as it really is. It was an abdication, if you like, from the big, difficult issues. Dylan was trying to get back home, to get on with the business of living.

I don't think he was doing it for any clearly defined philosophical reasons. He was driven to it by the need to survive and to find contentment. Bob Dylan himself said of the album: 'There's no attempt there to reach anyone but me.' This urge to be content, to be happy, to survive—if necessary at the expense of integrity—is something I believe to be characteristic of the seventies. It was a new self-centredness. And Dylan, was once again pointing the way.

The double album, *Self-portrait*, which contained a weird and wonderful personal selection including 'Blue moon', Paul Simon's 'The Boxer' and a heap of easy and apparently brainless tunes, was another piece of self-indulgence.

His next album *New morning* was better. Even so it was very 'down home'. The survival, self-perpetuation image was still strongly to the fore:

> 'Build me a cabin in Utah
> Marry me a kid
> Catch rainbow trout
> Have a bunch of kids who call me pa
> That must be what it's all about
> That must be what it's all about.'

More recently Dylan has started again. *Planet waves* and *Blood on the tracks* are stronger and much less Country-orientated. Some of the old Dylan images were beginning to show themselves again. *Blood on the tracks* came after the break-up of his marriage and it seems obvious that Dylan was once more uneasy with the world.

There seems to be a callous equation here. It's one that has often been made—good music cries out of pain, not ease. This is certainly true of Rock. The best music was the product of anger and rebellion. Even when the music sprang from optimism it was a fighting optimism, not a dead complacency. Dylan thought that a happy, rural family life was sufficient shelter from the world. But it proved too fragile a shelter to trust in and, when it blew away, the world was still there.

Desire and the subsequent live album *Before the flood* show Dylan has been playing the role of song-writer and musician, and not much more.

John Lennon's first, fully-fledged solo album after the Beatles broke up was *John Lennon and the Plastic Ono band*. It was nothing if not autobiographical. Lennon and Yoko Ono had been undergoing psychotherapy. They had had literally to re-enact the scenes of their first infant frustrations in order to isolate the first trauma. At the high point of frustration the patient gives vent to a 'primal scream'. The scream, in simple terms, was meant to be an uninhibited cleansing of the tensions that emanated from those early problems.

John Lennon's album was linked very closely to those therapy sessions; particularly relevant was a tortuous song about his early relationship with his mother. Having run the gauntlet of the whole Rock 'n' Roll generation, John Lennon ended up inside himself. The songs were about himself, or at least about himself and Yoko. He had started to explore his own world rather than the world around him.

Lennon, like Dylan, was a living example of the course of the Rock culture. He was no longer a Rock 'n' Roller, neither was he into love in the same way he had been, or as his notorious 'bed-ins' for peace were. He was no longer a leader—he had returned to the only thing he could believe in.

The song 'God' on his 1971 album expressed this in no uncertain terms: 'I don't believe in magic, I don't believe in Ching . . . Bible . . . Tarot . . . Hitler . . . Jesus . . . Kennedy . . . Buddha . . . Mantra . . . Gita . . . Yoga . . . Kings . . . Elvis . . . Beatles . . . Zimmerman . . . Beatles. I just believe in me, Yoko and me and that's reality.' He had catalogued just about all the influences he'd credited in interviews throughout his career. He'd turned his back on all of them.

The strands unravel

All the strands that went to make-up Rock were beginning to unravel. The heavy Rockers, the Country flavoured groups, and all the other elements were slowly separating.

Country is a good example. During the late sixties and early seventies, there had been a strong Country influence on Rock. As the idealism and the unity of the Rock culture faded, so Country music took off on its own. It would probably be true to say that Country Rock musicians simply carried on what they were doing. They became progressively more interested in their own brand of music. The same thing happened with the other strands of Rock music. Each developed its own sub-culture. Country bands were springing up all the time—The New Riders of the Purple Sage, Mike Nesmith's First National Country Band, The Flying Burrito Brothers, to name just a few.

Much of the music was impeccable. Songs tended to become vehicles for instruments and voices much more than for any particular message. Singer/song-writers such as Gram Parsons didn't altogether lose meaning. But, Parson's solo albums are very personal statements, about himself and his condition, rather than anything outside. Country Rock, left on its own lonely track, began to slip back into the sentimentality and musical cliché of the old Country mould. And what happened to Country music was repeated in several other areas of Rock music.

Hard and heavy

The central vein of Rock had been the vigorous, hard hitting, guitar-based Rock groups of the late sixties—bands like The Stones, The Who, Ten Years After, Johnny Winter, Steppenwolf and their contemporaries. Many of these groups built up a following with exciting acts on stage, and guitar pyrotechnics on record. The guitar and lead singer heroes personified by Clapton and Jagger were accorded genius status. These groups were what Rock was really about. They were seldom subtle but they were hard, fast and dealt in red-hot excitement. They could lift a crowd to its feet, making an audience dance, clap and roar its approval.

In the late sixties, Led Zeppelin came on the scene. With groups such as Deep Purple and Black Sabbath, they began

Led Zeppelin
'Took great delight in grinding out overtly sexual numbers'

to take hard Rock into a new dimension, Heavy Metal.

As the Rock culture foundered the emphasis turned from hard to heavy. There had always been sexual elements in Rock. It's impossible to see Jagger perform without understanding that. But it wasn't an obsessive preoccupation. Led Zeppelin were different, especially in their early days. They took great delight in grinding out overtly sexual numbers. 'Gonna give you every inch of my love' was one way of putting it. Heavy bands almost invariably built a song around a guitar riff which pounded out remorselessly and repeatedly until the ears were ringing. At the beginning this was sheer exuberance. By the end it was indulgence.

Led Zeppelin had certain undeniable musical qualities. But they were the exceptions. Horrendous, heavy, mind-deadening music was being generated by newcomers to the scene—Grand Funk Railroad, Black Widow, Status Quo (in their early manifestation), Blue Oyster Cult, Uriah Heep. It was more than loud. It was blacksmith music.

In Britain, in the early seventies, there was a phenomenon known to friends of mine as the 'greatcoat boys'. These were male teenagers with a marked taste for ex-air force and ex-army greatcoats—thick woollen garments that trailed the ground, with nickel-plated buttons and broad lapels. Jeans were often embellished with sewn-on patches bearing a variety of symbols and slogans. The girls preferred long Indian-print cotton dresses or jeans like those the boys wore. The greatcoat boys were the heavy music freaks.

Heavy music was a break from the Rock culture because it did not really follow the same direction as mainstream Rock. It was neither celebratory nor rebellious. It was therapeutic. It was body music and nothing more. It was a battering-ram against the senses. Heavy Rock audiences were only too willing to let themselves be pushed along. They offered themselves up to the music. They went to concerts with the specific intention of being zonked out. Heavy

Rock was escapist in a way that hard Rock hadn't been. Behind its posturings, hard Rock declared its resistance culture values. Heavy Metal was merely 'get down get with it'—a big suffocating blanket.

I think it is not coincidental that in both the States and Britain the seventies have seen a change in drug use. Among Rock audiences in particular, downers, (drugs that slow down the system) have become more popular than pep-pills. The use of alcohol has also increased. (During the drug-orientated days of the late sixties, alcohol was despised because it was a slowing, numbing agent, whereas grass and acid nudged the system alive and made users more aware of the possibilities of the universe.) In the seventies kids have been looking for oblivion, not vision.

Singer/song-writers

The personal and sensitive gifts of many singer/song-writers were an integral part of the Rock culture. Most of the solo performers who became popular in the late sixties and early seventies were, if not introspective, then at least very self-aware. The Folk boom started it. When the emphasis moved away from Protest, some performers were left wondering what to do next. Phil Ochs was a prime example. He carried on with Protest long after it was fashionable, zeroing in, particularly, on the Vietnam war. When the war ended his role disappeared. His sole purpose had been to fight. With no target his life fell to pieces. Finally he went to his sister's garage and hanged himself.

Others followed Dylan in singing more personal songs. The next generation of singers, though still in the Folk mould—tending to favour the single spotlight and acoustic guitar—were not protesters in the same sense as their predecessors. They might weep about the country, as Neil Young did in 'Alabama', or, like Joni Mitchell, berate those who would 'pull down paradise and put up a parking lot'.

But most of the time they made communicable songs out of their own experience of grief or joy.

Solo singers were at one time the only artists with any sort of grip on what was going on. While others were playing out Rock 'n' Roll parts, or degenerating into good-time music, singers like Jackson Browne were still saying something. He described the disillusion of Rock, for example, in a tremendous song, 'Before the deluge':

> 'On the brave and crazy wings of youth
> They went flying round in the rain
> And their feathers once so fine grew torn and tattered
> and in the end they traded their tired wings
> For the resignation that living brings.'

It was a sad epitaph. A bright and hopeful generation had sunk into decadence.

Others weren't so talented or so perceptive. Singers like Roy Harper positively wallowed in their own bitterness. Some, like James Taylor, sang finely crafted songs, at times really too personal and self-searching. There was an edge of introspection. Many of these songs were as therapeutic as they were communicative.

Singers began to make a meal of their private lives. For example, Carly Simon: 'You're so vain . . . Bet you think this song is about you.' Laura Nyro got deeper and deeper into her own private world. More recently Dory Previn has been prepared to bare her private life on stage and on record.

As the singer/song-writer role became popular, it also became less precise. Rod Stewart, who'd been hanging about the Rock scene for years, suddenly caught peoples' attention. Many of his songs were pleasant, interesting or quirky, but they didn't say a lot. He soon moved into spectacular Rock superstardom, but his songs remained the same—strong but hollow. The same could be said for

Carole King, perhaps one of the most craftsmanlike of all the song-writers. Out of this tradition have come singer interpreters like Joe Cocker, Judy Collins, Linda Ronstadt, Emmylou Harris and, with his other hat on, Rod Stewart. They are fine singers, most of them with great individual ability to make a song come alive. But few have had much to say. They are like actors, adapting readily to different parts—and entirely dependent on good material. Many of these interpreters have chosen to re-interpret older songs, partly because they have lived with and understood the old songs.

Glitter

All that was left, as the Rock culture disintegrated was 'the glitter and the rouge' (Jackson Browne's phrase).

David Bowie is the prime example. His brilliant use of different personae was a logical extension of Rock's own preoccupation with image. In the past, Rock performers had tended either to hide their vulnerability behind a public image or else to exaggerate certain natural characteristics. Bowie took the process one step further by manufacturing a whole series of different characters, each one a fantasy to be acted out, each one given his own musical style. It was sensationalism, drama with a veneer of meaning.

Bowie's fans reacted much more strongly to the image than to the music, although that cannot be discounted. Bowie is an excellent song-writer. His albums have always been full of originality. But they mirror only the image of the moment.

Lou Reed was the personification of the seamy side of New York life. He gloried in the Andy Warhol-dominated world of transvestites, junkies, male prostitutes, would-be-stars, hustlers, freaks and weirdos. His music, from the days with The Velvet Underground, has always been about that private, destructive world.

David Bowie
'His brilliant use of different personae was a logical extension of Rock's own preoccupation with image'

Alice Coopers' activities on and off stage were the product of a crass commercialism.

The decadence of the glitter was a short-lived flourish—a tired wave of a limp wrist. Francis Bacon, the painter, once said: '. . . all art has become a game by which man distracts himself. You may say that it always has been like that, but now it's entirely a game'.

The decadent image of David Bowie and Lou Reed was part of the same game-playing mentality. For the same reason that street kids go to extravagant lengths in order to subdue their boredom, decadence became a fad. It was something else to do; it was almost a ritual pushing over of sexual barriers. It had its repercussions among young people. For a time it was fashionable to be gay, or bi-sexual, or at least a bit effeminate. (For some reason butch women never received the same tolerance—perhaps they weren't decorative enough.)

It was tiresome and self-conscious and it never led anywhere. It was just one more symptom of the break-up of Rock culture.

Music for music's sake

Groups like Yes and Emerson, Lake and Palmer were self-conscious, like the decadents, but *ever* so serious. Once more they were committed to breaking down barriers—this time musical barriers. In this way Rock music joined up once again with the *avant-garde* music of the classical tradition. It has proved to be the same kind of dead-end.

The motivation behind this Classical Rock was the urge for musical development. In itself this was a good and healthy drive. But when it takes over and eclipses other considerations such as meaning or communication the music inevitably suffers. The group Yes have been particularly guilty of this. They have set out to explore the music in an attempt to extend its potential. It was a classic mistake.

Because they made experimentation the purpose, it was doomed to failure. Experiments do not necessarily produce results, original thinking or discovery. Yes have simply put themselves on an eternal hurdle course, hurdling for hurdling's sake.

A number of bands focus their musical attention on techniques and virtuosity, as distinct from anything the music might actually be *about*. ELP and The Soft Machine are good examples of extravagant but directionless accomplishment. Other examples are John McLaughlin's Mahavishnu Orchestra, Pink Floyd to some degree, and of course Rick Wakeman.

Another musical trend has been the wave of 'weeny-bopper' groups, Pop music tailored for kids: The Osmonds, Bay City Rollers, Slik and so on. They are inventions of the industry, carefully packaged and marketed. They carry on almost as if Rock 'n' Roll had never existed. During the decadent 'glitter' period, the Pop scene raised its junior commercial equivalents. T. Rex and Gary Glitter, dressed in satin and encrusted with sparkles, put on rather lame shows. It was empty, tired and contrived. Rod Stewart wasn't opposed to a bit of glitter—but he was a league above the rest. He had more style and was a better singer. His glamour became an accepted pose and meant nothing. He has put on his own spectacular—the Rod Stewart show.

There has always been a whole section of music which fits somewhere between Pop and Rock. It is well played, expensively recorded and says nothing. This has fed back into mainstream Pop. Artists like Elton John, who for a while was a promising Rock singer, suddenly became hit-single artists and international superstars. Elton John and Bernie Taupin have written good, classy hit songs, but they don't say a lot. Neither do many of the other artists, many of them successful in the Rock culture heyday of the sixties, who have regular chart success with well-crafted 'nothing' songs.

Chicago is one example; another is Fleetwood Mac. Yet another strand is good-time: a rash of bands and singers who have set out to entertain the troops. They have played pleasant, sometimes excellent, even hot music—but its always been a matter of having a good time. Billy Preston and Bobby Whitlock come into this category. The Faces, when Rod Stewart was with them, were the ace flyers of good-time. They were hot, exciting and thoroughly enjoyable—for the evening you saw them.

Survival

As inflation began to spiral, many young people who had previously rejected the idea of co-operation with straight society began in desperation to see what it had to offer. When the employment situation began to tighten, casual work, on which many young people depended, was the first to be hit. The seventies' economic squeeze made experimentation—whether in farming systems or a free lifestyle—less possible. People simply had to concentrate on survival.

Survival, rather than freedom, became the watchword. The seventies saw a new class emerge. It came out of the counterculture but no longer really subscribed to it. These people are the floaters: only vaguely 'alternative', vaguely left-wing, vaguely trendy and vaguely materialistic. Their strongest feature is their lack of positive commitment.

It is interesting to notice that in the recession economy, Rock groups, who earlier regarded the singles chart with dubious eye, began churning out single after single—in order to guarantee sales, guarantee an audience and guarantee survival.

So much has changed. In Britain for instance, the colleges and universities used to be an important circuit for Rock bands. There, more than anywhere else, the bands could play to their own audience—the new generation. The college circuit meant something. Now it no longer does, except in economic terms. It is just another gig with nothing particular to recommend it.

The group feeling and identity have gone. People still smoke dope but they do it for pleasure. It's no longer a symbol. It is the same with long hair. There is no particular reason to do one thing rather than another. What is important is to carry on.

Teenage rampage

Now, as I write Punk Rock/new-wave is the most talked-about phenomenon in the music press. It is undeniably exciting stuff. It has been a genuine and conscious attempt to bring music back into contact with its audience. Groups like the Sex Pistols and the Stranglers have gone on record as saying that the previous generation of Rock superstars have betrayed their fans by their tax exile, jet-set lifestyles and their flabby music.

The pundits and the record company PR boys have claimed that new-wave is the music of the dole queue, the product of high-rise flats—the image of the urban wasteland. This is partly true. Like early Rock 'n' Roll, Punk Rock, with its fast guitar chords pumped like pistons, its generally toneless vocals and slogan lyrics, carries much of the flavour of city life.

But it is not from the council estates that the initiative comes. In Britain, the art schools have, as always, produced some of the best exponents and manipulators of the Rock form. Malcolm McLaren, the manager of the Sex Pistols is an ex-art student, as was Pete Townshend, the mastermind of The Who. The Clash come from the same background. In Punk's shock tactics—the make-up, the fetish appendages, even the typography—there is a destructive artiness, echoes of the Dada anti-art movement of the early 1900s.

As for the dole queue, Johnny Rotten, the Sex Pistol's notorious lead singer said, 'I know it's tough on the dole,

Johnny Rotten
'In Punk's shock tactics there is a destructive artiness, echoes of the Dada anti-art movement of the early 1900s'

but it's not that bad. I was getting paid for doing nothing. I thought it was . . . great.' He was able to *use* the dole because a job was not what he wanted. He had his eyes on other things. Nevertheless, his audience may well look at the dole from a different point of view. If the new wave is not necessarily the product of unemployment, it does speak meaningfully to teenagers on the dole, or those who see unemployment in prospect. There is a great identification between the new-wave's audience and its performers, more so than there has been for a long time. The enthusiasm shown for this music is redolent of the Mod era. There is the same preoccupation with style, the same rejection of adult values.

New-wave has brought a spirit of adventure back to the music scene. Record companies can no longer afford to play safe. They are forced to experiment and take risks on unknown names—a departure that can do nothing but good for the industry in the long run. Perhaps the most exciting thing to happen is the effect of new-wave on the wider spectrum of Rock music. Punk began when it was repetitive and sameish. But it is bound to develop. There have already been groups influenced by new-wave. Others—for example Ian Dury, Graham Parker and the Rumour, Elvis Costello —who reject the banal, self-consciously nasty content of much of Punk, nevertheless share the vision for tough music which speaks realistically of *our* times.

'I matter'

Is there another Rock culture on the way? I don't think so. Exciting as much of the recent music has been, it is short on direction and on hope. Despite the righteous indignation directed at the selfish indulgence of past stars, new-wave is basically self-orientated.

Rock has always been partly about self, always a way of

saying, 'I matter'. But usually it has been balanced by a specific desire for freedom, love, peace, or a bigger slice of the future. New-wave is dedicated, it seems, only to the survival of *me*.

Punk Rock grew out of a mentality common in the big trade unions. Negotiation means applying industrial muscle. Demands are made by confrontation. The perennial question is, who has the whip hand if it comes to a fight?

The Punks in their early days used the same principle—it was a matter of making a big noise and getting noticed. If long hair was no longer shocking, then it would have to be safety pins, spitting and obscenities. The process is a tired spiral to nowhere. It is confrontation for no ultimate purpose.

Johnny Rotten, in 'Anarchy in the UK' sang, 'Don't know what I want, but I know how to get it'. He sums up the whole thing. Rock music is still powerful. It still has the potential to be the energy centre for change—but change to what?

Are we in for round after round of anger and recrimination? Are we, in future years, likely to see further waves of rebellion and self-assertion? Where does it all end?

The early Punks prided themselves on being hard-nosed realists. They saw no hope for the future. From their point of view they are right—but that doesn't give me or my thirteen-month-old daughter a lot to look forward to.

Discomania/Europop

The music of the discos and the top-forty radio shows is less challenging fare than new-wave. But if record sales are anything to go by, it accounts for the taste of a massive audience of young people. The disco scene is a subculture of its own. On Friday, Saturday and Sunday nights, a large proportion of western youth crowd into subterranean caves of one kind or another. The music is played mostly by black artists. It is mostly based on Soul and directed almost exclusively at the body. The appeal of the disco is escapist—to forget work, forget the cares of the real world and meet with others of like mind, and of the opposite sex, as the film *Saturday Night Fever* has shown only too well.

If anything, it is a more genuinely working-class music than new-wave. It is usually the brighter kids who go for the Ramones or the Stranglers. The street kids are down at 'Pebbles' or some such place. The groups are not the stars. The music and the audience are the draw.

The Europop sound of Abba and Demis Roussos is likewise contentless, escapist music. Its exponents, like the disco musicians, are realists—survivors. They know which side their bread is buttered. They will continue to exist by supplying the customer's needs, changing as the needs change. It is the old show-biz story.

The disco/Europop audience is feeding on nothing but its own need for good-time. Its very escapism makes it, in essence, as hopeless as the new-wave.

Jackson Browne in a recent album, with customary directness pinpoints the dilemma of the generation growing out of its twenties in the 1970s. In a song called 'The pretender' he looks back to the optimism of the sixties. He asks,

> 'What became of the changes we waited for love to bring?
> Were they only the fitful dreams
> of some greater awakening?'

He sings about day-to-day living, about how the dreams are gone leaving only a day-to-day survival 'with nothing to choose or to fight', caught between 'the longing for love and the struggle for the legal tender.'

In the end resignation wins: 'I'm gonna be a happy idiot and struggle for the legal tender'. True love, values and dreams can't match it. All the same its not a happy decision. Ideals are given up only with difficulty, but everyone has to live somehow. The end of the song tears me apart. It is so sad, so helpless, and it is so true of the present situation. Jackson Browne sings 'Are you there—say a prayer for the pretender, who started out so strongly only to surrender.'

It is a sad and a heavy thing that a movement of such hope and idealism should end this way; a great pretender, a failed attempt. On both sides of the Atlantic, youth were staking a claim for a new world. They couldn't sustain it. If man alone could shape his future it would have been different. Had he not been imperfect things would have changed. But that's not the way it is. Man, left to himself, will always fail. A rootless religionless generation alienated from reality and from God could do no more than fight gamely against the odds. It didn't make it. Hope—the only real hope, I believe—lies in the Christian understanding of man and his maker, in the Christian faith as the only effective basis for living in the real world. But the force which sprang from Rock remains the most exciting ideological movement that I have seen. 'Are you there, say a prayer for the pretender.'